LANDFILL

LANDFILL

Thomas Fasano

Coyote Canyon Press
Claremont, California

First Edition

Table of Contents

Whispers of the Mundane

In the whisper of leaves:
a subtle call, stirring:
drawing thoughts outward,
where light filters, gentle,
through the age-old boughs:
quiet life pulses.

Vines enwrap the oak:
entwined, they climb, seeking,
thrive on solar gifts,
ambition molded by
the contours of nature:
tales in green spirals.

Soft voices in dusk,
the slow simmer of life,
simple in its essence,
yet profound in scope:
bean by bean, the stew
builds in quiet strength.

Branches stretch skyward,
not to conquer but to
embrace the air: free
yet rooted deeply,
an anchored resilience:
growth in constraint.

Through the cool pane I watch:
leaves rustle, a quiet hymn
about simplicity's truth,
a testament to the
sufficiency in small things:
breath, being, belonging.

Outside, a cosmos in motion,
inside, a heart beats measured:
each tick a stilled echo
of somber understanding,
the basic sustenance of soul
found in everyday rhythms.

Each day spills over:
the next, a parade of minutes,
each hour teeming with
the potential of the unnoticed,
every task a stanza
in life's long poem.

The soybeans' soft whisper:
simmering, they speak of
easement, of the mend
from hunger's sharp edge:
how tender simplicity
feeds the depths of us.

A leaf detaches, falls:
a slow dance to the ground,
each twirl a quiet drama,
a lesson in letting go,
the peace found in surrender,
the beauty of descent.

As twilight deepens,
the world sheds its colors:
grey shades infiltrate,
bringing a balance of
understanding: dimming light,
brightening insight.

Indeed, why should ambition
push us to burn so brightly
that we miss the soft glow
of life's gentle fire?
Why reach for the sun
when warmth is right here?

In every modest action,
a grandeur unfolds subtly:
the brushstroke on canvas,
the words that teach kindness,
the meals that nourish:
all small, all infinite.

My years—like the tree—
grow rings hidden beneath
bark's sturdy insistence,
every layer a silent
witness to seasons lived,
storied in its grain.

The whispers wind around,
tight and insistent,
reminders of things undone,
a duty, heavy yet hollow,
echoes in silent chambers,
vines curling tighter.

My chair, a cradle of thought,
contemplates these intrusive sighs,
while outside, the wind speaks,
a softer, gentler plea,
trees bowing with the grace,
of seasons changing ceaselessly.

Their leaves, a rustle of truths,
broadcast across the sky's arc,
saying growth isn't just a reach
but also a settling in,
an acceptance of the pace
at which life unfolds.

I turn and survey my room:
every corner a story told,
the stretches of paint,
    the well-thumbed books,
each a quiet testament
to the life I have fashioned.

In the kitchen, the aroma
of simmering soybeans fills the air,
  a simple dish, unadorned yet rich,
speaking of the earth's gifts,
   their plainness misleading,
    a complex dance of sun, soil, rain.

How then to measure the weight
of existence? By the clamor
  of accolades, or the silent nod
    of a day well spent,
in the hum of ordinary joy
    that does not seek the sun?

Through the window,
the branches tell their tales,
    sprawled against the backdrop
of a twilight sky, serene,
whispering of endurance,
of beauty in the bounded.

And isn't this the grand canvas,
more vivid than any dreamt ambition?
Where each small act,
each quiet moment,
builds a legacy not of monuments,
but of moments breathed fully.

The call of legacy, once loud,
now fades, a dim star in the dusk,
outshone by the brilliance
of the mundane, its soft glow
a surer light by which to see,
a gentler path to tread.

For the greatness sought in youth,
now seems a different hue,
colored by the strokes
of brushes dipped
in the palette of daily living,
each mundane chore a stroke of art.

Outside, the night has deepened,
and the trees sway with secrets,
the silent understanding that
to stand firm, roots entwined
with the earth's own heart,
is to know the truest growth.

And so, as whispers of ambition
dissolve into the quiet dark,
I find the grandeur not in the distant
but right here, in the simmer,
in the paint's slow drying,
in the silent knowing of the trees.

Each day, each act, a poem,
crafted not for the world's stage,
but for the quieter theaters
of kitchens, gardens, quiet walks,
where the grand acts are small,
and the small acts, grand.

In this twilight of years,
not a dimming, but a blending,
where light merges with shadow,
and what was once urgent
gives way to the gentle pull
of a life rich in unnoticed poetry.

The legacy not a loud echo,
but a soft sigh, a murmur
of leaves and whispered winds,
a life lived in the soft margins,
where the grandest poems are lived,
not written, but deeply felt.

Thus, I sit, the night around me,
a cloak woven of starlight and peace,
and know that the vines of ambition,
once sharp and insistent,
have loosened their grip,
swayed by the wiser whispers of trees.

Each breath a stanza,
each day a line in the poem
of a life quietly splendid,
where the measure of its verse
is the love it contains,
the peace it bestows.

And as I rise from the chair,
the room settled around me,
I carry the quiet assurance
that this, here, now,
is the poem I was meant to write,
the life I was meant to live.

In the simple acts,
the grandeur I sought
finds its true form,
not in the pages of a book,
but in the gentle legacy
of living well and quietly.

In this serene acceptance,
the invasive whispers fade,
overcome by the richer sounds
of life's subtle rhythms,
the heartbeat of a home,
the breath of the natural world.

As the night deepens further,
I embrace the enveloping dark,
rich with the poetry
of a life unspoken,
where the greatest verses
are those lived, not written.

And I sleep, dreams mingling
with the realities of day,
each a soft reflection
of the other, a poem
composed in the quiet night,
enduring in the echo of stars.

In the dim light of morning,
the fresh page of a new day,
I find poetry in the simplicity,
the grandeur not in what is done,
but in the grace of the doing,
the beauty of being.

Thus, the vines of ambition,
once constrictors of thought,
now lie tranquil,
a part of the landscape
of a life where the true poem
is the living itself.

As the day unfolds,
its hours like verses
written in the light of the sun,
I walk the paths of routine,
each step a line,
each breath a rhyme.

In this lyrical living,
the mundane becomes magic,
the everyday an elegy
to the profound simplicity
of existing not for the poem,
but as the poem itself.

Amidst the chores, the walks,
the meals shared in quiet joy,
each moment stretches,
a canvas where the colors
of ordinary brilliance
paint the truest masterpiece.

And when evening returns,
its soft curtain closing another day,
I rest in the solace
        that my life, my art, my poem,
resides not in the words I write,
but in the life I weave.

So weaves the night,
its dark threads mingled
with the light of fading stars,
a tapestry of twilight musings,
where the grandest thoughts
are those most quietly kept.

And I, a scribe of the subtle,
find my pen stilled,
my heart full,
in the knowledge that
the finest poetry
is that which lives and breathes.

In this quiet culmination,
the whispers finally hushed,
I see the grandeur not as a peak
to be scaled, but as a valley
to be walked, deeply and truly,
where the paths are lined with the poetry

of everyday existence.
In the end, the greatest poem
may not be one that is written,
but one that is lived,
each day a verse,
each act a word,

each breath a metaphor.
For in the simplicity of living,
in the quietude of being,
there lies the profound,
the truly grand,
where the smallest details

sing the sweetest songs.
And so the poem flows,
a river of quiet moments
and simple pleasures,
meandering through the landscape
of a life where the mundane

is touched with magic.
Each morning a new stanza,
each evening a line concluded,
in the ongoing poem
of a life lived quietly,
where the most resonant verses

are those least noticed.
In the gentle cycle of days,
the poetry of existence
unfolds in soft whispers,
a quiet conversation
between the soul and the world,

a dialogue of breath and being.
Here, in the twilight of years,
the grandeur once sought
finds its true voice,
not in the clamor of achievement,
but in the silent symphony

of a life well-lived.
And as the seasons turn,
each bringing its own verse,
the poem of my days
takes shape in the hush of hours,
each tick of the clock

a quiet punctuation.
In this rhythm, I find
 the poetry I sought,
not in the words I write,
but in the life I live,
 where the grandest verses

are woven from the quietest threads.
 Thus, the days pass,
 each a soft addition
to the poem of years,
where the simplest moments
 become the stanzas

most cherished.
In the end, the whispers fade,
replaced by the deeper truth
that the greatest poetry
is found not in striving,
but in simply being,

in the quiet heart of the mundane.
As the final lines are lived,
the poem complete
in its quiet splendor,
I rest in the knowing
that what I sought

has been here all along,
in the gentle art of living.
The whispers keep me:
late in the hour,
reflecting on whether
ambition is my friend

or a wayward siren:
the room's quiet hum
aligns with my heartbeat,
each pulse a gentle echo
of simpler, more honest days,
when dreams were seeds

waiting for the right
season to bloom:
not rushed by the fierce
hunger of youth, but
steadied by the patience
of age, understanding

the beauty in waiting:
the soybeans simmer
noiselessly, their soft skins
taut with potential,
silent witnesses to the
value of the unhurried:

nature teaches, much
like the trees, growth
is a testament not to speed
but endurance:
each leaf, a page
of history.

Entropic Echoes

Here at the edge of decay:
the air thins with the cry
of gulls: where waste sculpts
landscapes: columned high,
weighed down by the tonnage
of our neglect: a heavy truth:

Could we breathe deeply—
from the shadows cast by
our mountainous excess?
The flutter: wings in ash-grey,
circling: predatory upon these
cast-off remnants of days:

Fragments: fractured plastics,
glint beneath the sun, crafting
a mosaic of the unwanted:
all here: the thrown-away,
resigned to outlive us, a slow
dance of the undying stuff:

Upon this altar of leftovers,
paths worn by scavengers,
both living and mechanical,
they weave through the relics
of rapid consumption, seeping
into earth's battered veins:

A bottle lies: label faded, sun-bleached,
its once-shiny surface dulled
by the smear of time: potions
once valued, now just hollow
echoes of former needs —
the castoff chemistry binding:

Tires piled like pyres await
ignition: rubber and wire meshed
in silent testament to movement
now stilled: these are the black
rings of modern ritual, less smoke
more residue: entropic echoes:

Every mound a manuscript,
written in debris: our narrative,
compressed: plastics, organics,
metals intertwine: telling tales
of quick fixes and quicker discards,
the lore of disposability etched deep:

We layer the earth with our discards,
thin strata that speak to hurry,
the sediment of the unnecessary,
compelled by the whispered
promise of the new: regeneration
shadowed by its own abundance:

In this, the refuse speaks: not just
of endings, but of beginnings:
of cycles turned vicious,
where creation stems from
the fullness of voids,
where to discard is to distribute:

A newspaper flutters, trapped
in the wind's capricious hold,
its headlines blurred, a smudged
reminder of yesterday's urgencies,
now wrapping today's fish, scent
of ink and decay intertwined:

And still, the gulls circle, eager
for the remnants of this feast,
their cries slicing through the
droning rumble of compactors,
nature's cleanup crew, picking
        at the carcass of consumerism:

  Look closely: for in this heap,
ideas ferment: the discarded
      seeds of tomorrow's blooms,
growth fertilized by the folly
of excess: the earth reclaims
its due, one discarded bit at a time:

These heaps: not just end,
but also passage: from form
to formlessness: and back again,
material journeys echoing
        in the space between buying
and the burial of the used:

Each piece discarded carries
        a footprint: oil, metal, water,
    expended in creation, now
lie stagnant in these hills,
the latent energy of what's left
a murmuration of potentials:

Through the rot and rust,
    continuity: elements break,
recombine: nothing lost but
shape: the atoms that built
   the screen, the cup, the can,
embark on new assignments:

This scene of decay, also
  a cradle: where what is discarded
gestates into tomorrow's soil,
our refuse, our rejected
atoms: ready to be reborn,
instructed by the necessity of cycles:

Here we stand, pondering
this panorama: the landscape
crafted of our own unmaking,
wondering at the scale of our
footprints: and how to tread,
from here, more lightly: in concert:

A lesson in endings and
beginnings: continuous as the
turning earth beneath a canopy of waste,
the importance of what we let fall
  away: not just the object, but
  the idea of its necessity dissipates:

  Each discarded element—a
silent summons to rethink,
reshape how we live,
the way we bind our lives
    to things, the weight of
    our desires pressing deep:

    Towers of refuse rise:
plastic gleam, metal shards,
    scattered remnants
of yesterday's haste,
    forgotten functions
  whisper into wind.

A colony of gulls
sweeps over: harsh cries,
webbed feet never touching
the sin of discarded things,
each dive: a judgement,
or merely survival?

The rust, the rot, the rancor:
decay is a teacher.
Look, how products once prized
meld into mountains,
and mountains gradually wear,
layer by layer.

Lids, cups, rags:
splayed like wildflowers,
beauty in repulsion,
stark contrasts that force
our eyes, compel minds
to see worth anew.

Here we uncover:
the skeletal remains
of our feast on the earth,
each bone picked clean,
every marrow sucked dry:
silent, damning evidence.

Yet, amid spoil and spoilage,
a sprouting seed: hope
or stubborn defiance?
Nature asserts her vim,
green-shoots piercing
through thin veils of plastic.

Crushed cans glitter
like jewels in rough,
the sun strikes, transforms
what was thrown, abandoned,
into a tableau vibrant
with unintended hues.

Rumbles of machines
in the distance, coming
to bury, to make new room,
constant cycles turning:
what we cast away, buried,
will one day be unearthed.

We stand, complicit,
at the altar of excess,
offering more than we are,
taking less than we could,
every discard a prayer,
every collection, confession.

Particles, atoms, at odds:
the smallest elements rebel,
breaking bonds, forming
new alliances in the secrecy
of soil, unseen, yet
working vast transformations.

A child's broken toy,
faded, split, eye missing:
once cherished, now part
of the detritus: does it recall
the warmth of hands,
the echo of laughter?

This heap, this shrine,
a meditation on endings,
but also on beginnings:
for in every termination
there lies a kernel,
latent with new birth.

Lament not just for loss,
but marvel at the persistence
of matter: nothing lost,
everything transformed,
in the vast crucible
of existence, transmutation.

We discard so lightly,
what was held dear,
forgotten in the turn
of days, the rush
of new desires,
the relentless push for more.

But here, in this decay,
insistence: a reminder,
that what is thrown away
carries stories, weight,
the accumulated charge
of lives in passage.

Each bottle, scrap, fragment,
a manuscript of human want,
a testimony to the brief flare
of possession, the swift
passage to the irrelevant,
the dated, the obsolete.

Yet, in obsolescence,
   a peculiar dignity:
each item a chapter
in the grand narrative
   of consume and cast,
   an endless repeat.

As the sun arcs lower,
shadows stretch, like fingers,
drawing out the lines
of connection, of consequence,
from the personal
to the planetary.

The refuse, a repository,
a lexicon of discard,
each term defined not
merely by its ending,
but by its place in
  a continuum of renewal.

Air heavy with the musk
of degradation, yet
wafting, too, the crisp scent
    of opportunity,
       of lessons learnt,
hard, but necessary.

We linger, reluctant,
drawn to the repulsion,
to the sheer scale of our
own creation, the refuse
     of millennia in making,
       a legacy of leftovers.

Yet, even here, beauty,
if beauty it can be called,
in the resilience of rejection,
in the sheer tenacity
of discarded dreams,
    refusing to vanish quietly.

In this landscape of loss,
where detritus dominates,
a quiet call to attention,
to the siren of simplicity,
the need to stem the tide
of endless acquisition.

    For in every unwanted heap,
in every neglected pile,
  a story of excess,
    a parable of plenty,
a caution to the wind,
a challenge to change.

We stand, thus, reflective,
  among relics of our own making,
pondering the paths of things
we thought to shed,
    only to find them returned,
mirrored back at us.

Here, in this temple of trash,
a sermon in every scattered
  piece, a lesson in every
layer uncovered,
the past speaking
to a possible future.

Each step on crumpled remnants
a step across epochs,
crossing boundaries of behavior,
from consumption to contemplation,
from neglect to respect,
a full circle made.

The refuse: our manuscript,
written not in ink,
but in leftovers,
the unwanted, the used,
calling us to read,
to understand, to act.

As the day yields
to dusk, light dims,
casting long shadows
over human landscapes,
illuminating our follies,
softening our faults.

We depart, but carry
with us the residue,
not just on soles,
but in souls, the imprint
of a pilgrimage to
the heart of habit.

Change whispers
amongst the waste,
a subtle shift,
like the softest breeze
hinting at storms,
at the stirrings of renewal.

This refuse, not just remnants
but reminders,
each piece echoing
a potential for redemption,
for rebirth from rejection,
for beauty born of neglect.

The gulls circle,
persistent in their patrol,
as night claims the heaps,
and we, turning home,
carry a new awareness,
a burden turned blessing.

A final glance back,
the rubbish less random,
more a mosaic,
each part positioned
in a play of purpose,
of possibility, of pause.

Thus, we reconsider
what to cast off,
what to hold close,
the weight of waste,
the worth of wanting less,
the wisdom found in remains.

Endings here are openings,
trash transformed to treasure,
the rejected, revered,
a cycle seen complete,
in the turning of earth,
in the tilting of minds.

In mounds of decay, where
   papers flutter like lost wings:
here lies our yesterday,
discarded: crumpled,
      forgotten like a thought
      lost amid the mind's rush.

Plastic glints, a mockery
   of permanence: it shapes
  the earth as much as clay,
  clogged in the spirit's drain,
polluting what we consider
pristine, untouched.

Rusted metals, rebar bones,
peek from heaps like relics
      of a techno-driven zeal:
our era's skeletons, stripped
of flesh, speak to us
in the harsh tongue of rust.

An albatross of waste, circling,
finds not fish, but bags,
billowing silent in the blue:
a testament to appetites,
   swallowed whole, returning
to haunt our ocean dreams.

Circuit boards, silicon souls,
left to leech their leaden tales
into the thirsty soil:
do they dream, I wonder,
of a silicon resurrection,
bytes blooming into consciousness?

Cycle of Neglect

In the twist of metal, sharp
edges gleam: dusk's light
catches every angle here,
in this space abandoned:
once filled, now emptied—
specters whisper of use lost.

Rust sings its slow song,
a hymn of decay: it creeps
along the old pipes, vines
of oxidation bloom, intricate,
infusing air with stories of
slow surrender and retreat.

Tires stacked, a rubber mound,
monuments to journeys ended,
each layer a silent testament
to miles traveled, paths once
etched across the earth's skin,
now still, quiet, stacked aside.

Plastic sheens under sun's glare,
crinkling, cracking as it ages,
brittle fragments scatter:
a mosaic of our making,
littering Earth's broad lap,
witness to the excess.

The ground, soaked in oil,
glistens with a rainbow sheen,
a beauty born from spoil,
nature absorbs, adapts—
we observe, noting how life
tends to reclaim, to cover.

Wires dangle, loop, entwine,
electric veins now powerless,
conduct no more the current
that animated the old cores,
now silent, the flow stemmed,
broken circuitry of progress.

In these remnants of function,
the skeleton of industry bares
its bones: steel beams jut
against the sky, stark, cold,
pointing like fingers blaming
us for the swift departure.

Shattered glass like stars
scattered on the dirt,
reflecting light, broken
yet each shard still sharp,
cutting through illusions,
revealing truths buried.

Concrete cracks where grass:
audacious, pushes upward,
nature's resilience displayed
in each determined sprout,
fighting for sunlight, for air,
in defiance of human intent.

Amid decay, a flower blooms,
unexpected vibrant defiance,
like hope that springs so fierce
from depths of direst despair,
splashes color on the grey,
life asserting, persisting.

Wind whispers through frames,
empty windows channeling
voices of the past, carried
on breezes that traverse
the abandoned corridors,
ghosts of laughter, cries.

Each piece discarded links
to the other: a chain of refuse,
tying one error to another,
a history of consumption
written in the littered layers,
pages in the dirt, unfurled.

Here the earth accepts each
offering we have cast off,
turning detritus to dust,
digesting slowly each mark
left by our hands, our haste,
in its vast, patient stomach.

Continuing, the wind picks up,
carrying scents of salt, of iron,
mingling with the soft decay,
a perfume of human living
and dying, of constructing
and deconstructing, endlessly.

Water collects in hollows,
puddles mirroring sky's face,
clouds drift over, silent,
watching their reflection
disturbed by a thrown stone,
ripples reaching out, fading.

Underfoot, the crunch of gravel,
each step a disturbance,
a sound that marks presence
    in a place where absence
reigns, where silence gathers
like dust, thick and blanket-like.

Amidst these shadows of past,
    the sun breaks through cracks,
  illuminating what's left behind,
    highlighting the beauty in
the abandoned, the discarded,
    finding worth in the worthless.

  This dance of light and shadow,
a ballet performed on stages
of concrete, glass, and steel,
    choreographed by time and
neglect, yet each movement
tells of life's stubborn pulse.

  What lessons lie among these
    ruins, messages etched in rust,
  written in the webs of weeds?
Can we learn from what we
    leave behind, seeing not just
endings but potential starts?

  Staring at this jumble of past,
    conscious of the crunch under
each hesitant step, I feel
the weight of my own waste,
the heavy echo of my tread
on the beaten, burdened earth.

We walk on, threading through
this labyrinth of leftovers,
each turn a reminder of
what we discard, what endures,
how nature claims, cleanses,
and corrects our careless drop.

Musings meld with the material,
thoughts tangled in the tangible,
a meditation on the mergings
where man's marks meet
the mute, enduring patience
of a world too wise to waste.

Reflections ripple, rebound,
off metal, glass, water,
each surface a mirror
to our actions, reactions:
do we see ourselves here,
in this stillness, this decay?

The echo of a distant crash,
something collapses, gives way,
a reminder that all is transient,
that even the strongest structures
submit to time's tireless gnawing,
and every thing must fall.

Yet in falling, a freeing:
spaces open, possibilities
emerge, nature nibbles
at the edges of our errors,
crafting compost from
the carcasses of our creations.

Again, the cycle spins:
destruction breeds creation,
    decay seeds the soil for
new growth, and we,
watchers and participants,
  learn to see beauty in the breaking.

Seasons cycle, sun to storm,
time ticks through the trash,
teaching us in its tireless way
    that nothing is truly static,
everything moves, morphs,
  matters in its moment.

Time, the great teacher,
shows us the steps to take,
from ruin rises renewal,
from discarded dreams
spring seeds of new days,
planted in the past's rich loam.

Connections clear between
the cracked and the whole,
each fragment a piece of
a larger puzzle, shaping
the image of tomorrow
from the shards of yesterday.

Here, amidst the refuse, we see
  not just the end but beginnings,
  a cyclic renewal where even
the most abject elements hold
the potential for transformation,
    recycling despair into hope.

Sixty times these thoughts weave,
through lines of loss and layers
of leaving, arriving always
at the truth of change,
the enduring cycle that spins
from refuse to reclamation.

Thus, we tread on, thinkers
and doers, destroyers and creators,
bound by our blunders, buoyed
by our betterments, always
bending towards balance,
learning to live with our leavings.

This is the spindle of energy,
the ceaseless motion that moves
all forms back to the force
from which they sprung—
our shared imperfections,
our profoundest chances for connection.

Beneath the rusted iron,
the forgotten plastic:
scattered and strewn
like autumn's lost leaves —
here, the ground murmurs:
dark soil fermenting

beneath the refuse,
the slow pulse
of a world unseen,
working, weaving:
roots navigating
through compacted scrap,

finding life in the loam
of discarded things,
the transformation hidden
but potent as dawn:
acid rain whispers
to the crumbling rebar,

a chemical caress
that speaks of change,
decay that nourishes,
erosion as a form of care:
stars appear above
fields of spent metal —

they, too, are fires
of transformation,
alight with the glow
of fusion and fission:
amidst such vast cycles,
I stand, breathing in

the tang of decay,
the alchemy of air
turning filth into breath,
the rank into renewal:
each atom connected
in this dance of particles —

from dust to dust,
but gloriously reused,
a continuum of matter
that refuses stasis:
these processes
mirror our lives,

our errors layered
  thick as the deposits
underfoot: each misstep
a sediment of learning:
how we've shaped
this world with hands

eager and blind,
how it shapes us back,
compressing us under
the weight of consequences:
   yet, in this pressing,
a diamond emerges:

insights hard-pressed
from the pressures
of existence, clarity
carved out of chaos:
these fragments,
      jagged and raw,

tell of a beauty
inherent in the broken,
potential in what's passed
   over, ignored, left behind:
the squirming earthworms
beneath our feet,

      architects of recovery,
turning waste into wealth,
  the soil's dark gold,
rich with redemption:
as the moon rises,
reflecting off shards

of shattered glass,
it does not scorn
  the sharpness,
but bathes it in silver:
light that finds all crevices
  and creases, not to expose

    but to illuminate
  the beauty in the scars,
the purpose in the pieces,
the whole in the broken:
thus, in this communion
of decay and growth,

I find a profound unity,
  a shared pulse beneath
the apparent ruin,
a symphony in the trash:
each discarded component,
every rusty nail sings

    of connection,
the threads that bind us
    in a web of mutual need,
of collective becoming:
on this edge of despair,
  I perceive not an end,

but a beginning,
the continuous loop
of matter and meaning,
the endless engagement:
the cycle swirls around,
  from the highest star

to the deepest dump,
spinning stories
of transformation,
of energy never lost,
but eternally transformed:
here, amidst the echoes

of past follies,
a future whispers,
promising not purity,
but a patchwork perfection,
a quilt stitched from remnants:
and I step lightly,

honoring each piece,
feeling the hum
of the earth's deep diurnal
rhythms, the beat
of regeneration, ongoing:
this is the consciousness

that spans continents,
a shared breath in the smog,
a collective sigh in the soil,
binding us in our blunders,
teaching us through decay:
and so, I watch the horizon,

where the sun hints
at tomorrow's rise,
a new day spun from
the old, a narrative
woven from wear:
and I am thankful

for this place,
    this moment of clarity
in the clutter,
where each dropped
    can, each worn tire,
is a call to contemplation,

a meditation on connection,
  on the relentless reinvention
of the world, and ourselves
within it: for here
    lies not just the problem,
but also the solution,

etched in the debris,
  singing in the soil,
dancing in the decay,
  an eternal invitation
to see, to understand,
to engage deeply:

and in this participation,
  we find not just healing,
but a profound homecoming,
a return to the essentials,
stripped of excess,
rich in the essentials,

where every end is also
a beginning, every loss
a potential gain,
  and each goodbye
carries the seed
  of a new hello.

Cosmic Choreography

atoms dance unseen:
their rhythms, a mystery
  I ponder, silent
edges of petals
    begin to whisper secrets:
photosynthesis

    sunlight converts to
    energy, life's currency
fed by a bright touch
particles merge and
divide: a cosmic ballet
in infinite space

    vibrations hint at
hidden forces that shape us,
as we shape the world
nature's blueprint, vast,
intricately detailed, yet
full of blank spaces

the boulder: still, yet
alive with ancient atoms,
quietly telling
its history: each
  layer a testament to

persistent change
fossils entombed in
stone—silent narrators of
  earth's forgotten tales
erosion crafts new
landscapes, slowly sculpting the

future from the past
water carves its path,
a soft persistence that wears
away even stone
mountains echo with
the stories of the earth's deep,

unyielding heartbeat
staring into skies,
pondering the vast cosmos,
I find solace there
stars, scattered like dust,

each a furnace of secrets,
burning to be known
light travels across
emptiness to touch my eye:
a connection made
galaxies spin in

majestic indifference
to human concerns
cosmic dance unfolds,
each movement led by physics,
but who cues the band?
formation, collapse:

the universe pulses with
creation, decay
leaves rustle: whispers
of the wind's passing secrets,
shared with open air

each leaf, a vessel
for sunlight, water, and air,
synthesizing life
roots delve into earth,
anchoring life's expanse in
the fertile darkness

branching out, trees form
networks of living wood—
communities thrive
cycles of seasons
mirror the cycles within,
each end a new start

growth and decay: the
eternal rhythm playing
through each living thing
behold the river:
its course defined, yet always

shifting, adapting
water's fluid grace,
teaching the strength found in yielding,
the power of flow
streams join and expand,
gathering force, carving new

paths through resistance
rocks smoothed by passage,
remnants of resistance lost
to persistent waves
the river knows no
stagnation: only onward,

always becoming
  creation's essence,
 etched in every droplet's path,
mirrors our own search
energy binds us,

invisibly connecting
atom to cosmos
 the wind's unseen push,
the pull of the earth beneath,
forces that bind us
   heat from a fire,

radiating warmth, shared
like a common breath
electric currents,
   sparking innovations, light
our darkened spaces
magnetism: unseen

   attraction, guiding, pulling,
  a force to reckon
energy cycles,
  in and out, a breath of life
sustaining us all

contemplation leads
me to the edge of knowing,
where questions flourish
mind meets matter in
a dance of curious steps,
exploring edges

thoughts fray like thread, pulled
apart by the tension of
discovery's weight
knowledge: a construct
built on the framework of doubt,
always expanding

each revelation
leads to deeper mysteries,
endless corridors
understanding's path,
winding and unpredictable,
beckons me forward

microscopic worlds,
unseen yet integral to
the fabric of life
cells divide, each split
a decision, a precise

execution of plans
genetic codes, like
ancient texts, hold the secrets
of life's continuance
enzymes catalyze,
accelerating the dance

of biochemicals
life's complexity,
hidden in simplicity,
a paradox held
within each cell, a
universe of activity,

silent yet vibrant
atoms to systems,
each scale reveals a layer
of deeper intrigue
from quarks to quasars,

the universe layers its
mysteries in scales
hidden dimensions,
perhaps beyond our grasp, yet
tantalizing close
theories converge,

diverge, a scientific
dialogue unfolds
reality's fabric,
stretched by our probing minds,
reveals its elastic
nature's laws, written

in the language of math, yet
poetry at heart
pondering the vast,
I'm dwarfed by the infinite,
yet integral too

like a single note
in an endless symphony,
distinct yet blended
existence—a thread
woven through time's vast tapestry,
colorful, vibrant

engaged in the dance
  of creation, observer
and participant both
seeking connections,
finding patterns in the chaos,
as stars find their orbits

my thoughts, like planets,
revolve around the bright sun
   of curiosity
      pausing to reflect,
I see the interplay of

light and shadow play
dawn's early light breaks,
  scattering night's shadows with
a gentle assertion
the cycle of day
and night, a visual

metaphor for thought
insights, like sunbeams,
sometimes pierce the clouded mind,
illuminating
the twilight of doubt
gives way to the clarity

of understanding
  evening's cool descent,
  a time for quiet reflection,
    gathers twilight thoughts
walking paths worn smooth

by the passage of many,
  I tread thoughtfully
each step a touch upon
the earth, a moment shared
with all who've passed here
the trail winds ahead,

its course as unknown as our
own future footsteps
paths diverge, choices:
each direction offers its
own mysteries, gifts
following the flow,

I trust the journey's wisdom,
  guided by instinct
the destination,
    less vital than the lessons
learned with each step taken

  contemplating the
ebb and flow of existence,
life's tides rise and fall
    each wave a heartbeat,
each tide the breath of the world,
  inhaled and exhaled

oceans, vast and deep,
hold secrets in their saline
depths, ancient, preserved
the pull of the moon,
a dance of celestial
attraction and grace

tides sculpt the shorelines,
softening edges, drawing
new forms in the sand
sandcastles erode,
reminding us: all is transient,
yet endlessly renewed

thus, I stand, witness
to the unfolding of time,
its relentless stride
moments, like water,
slip through the fingers, yet leave

a residue of wisdom
the present, a gift
that is perpetually
unwrapping itself
  time's river carries
us forward, through landscapes both

familiar and new
    the past, a riverbank
eroded by memory's flow,
shaped by the current
future, an ocean
awaiting exploration,

    boundless and unknown
pondering the thread
   that connects macro to micro,
    woven through it all
      from the cosmic web

to the neural networks deep
    within our own minds
patterns recur, like
themes explored in variations
across time and space
   chaos and order,

    randomness and pattern, a
continuum of scale
nature's fractals, self-
similar at different
levels of being
  understanding this,

the universe seems less vast,
more like a known path
  as I reflect on
the interconnectedness,
   complexity thrives

each part dependent
on another, a web of
  symbiotic threads
life, a mosaic
composed of infinite
interacting pieces

biodiversity
   provides resilience, each
     species a strong thread
disruption teaches
the value of each component,
     integral to the whole

humility borne
from recognizing our role,
not dominators, but part
throughout this journey,
each observation a step

toward deeper truths
the mundane becomes
a window into the profound,
each detail magnified
perception shifts, like
prisms bending light, revealing

spectra hidden within
questioning is more
important than the answers
found along the way
each inquiry a
guiding light, illuminating

paths through dark unknowns
knowledge, once a shore,
now becomes a horizon,
ever expanding
thus concludes my walk

through landscapes both grand and
intimate, profound
awareness expanded,
each discovery a pulse
in the rhythm of growth
the beauty of this,

continuous unfolding,
lies in the journey
not just destination,
but the steps along the way,
each a story told
immersed in the dance

of cosmos and quarks, I am
both lost and found anew
standing at the edge,
ready to dive back into
the great unknown sea
atoms split and fuse:

quarks swirl in hidden hues,
the dance of part to whole,
echoing the scroll
of universe, inscribed
in the fold of tides.
boulders not just stone,

but records, deeply sown
of ages in their core,
silent, yet they roar
of pressures, heat, the dance
of earth in its advance.
the lab's sharp light gleams,

slashes through the dreams
of matter as merely dead,
revealing, instead,
vibrations: the pulse,
life's unseen, vast impulse,
each measurement taken.

Temporal Scars

Amid shouts and metal clangs:
    the earth turns anew,
its green whispers lost
beneath the tread of progress.
Silent, I stand, a witness
    to the once wild, now tamed.

The commissioner, outlined
against a backdrop of steel,
directs with gestures
that carve air into submission:
this land, reshaped,
    bears the scars of new visions.

  Heavy wheels compress,
grounds that once sprouted
wildflowers and secrets;
now secrets are buried
    deeper than roots:
  hidden, yet persisting.

Birds trace the sky,
their shadows fleeting
over landscapes forever changed.
I watch, pondering the flight—
  is it escape or just another
circular return to the altered?

Each dump of waste,
    like sediment layers,
    builds the foundation of
tomorrow's archaeology;
  future relics of our consumption,
cataloged in refuse.

With every shove of soil,
the notion of permanence
falters, collapses into
the temporality of man's creation:
what we build over,
nature quietly reclaims.

The stink of effort and decay
mingles with cold air;
even the winter sun seems
to squint, dimmed by
the dust of our ambitions,

dull against the clamor.
Clouds, like watchers,
hang low, draped in grey;
their judgment, silent
as if even the sky can't
decide whether to weep

or merely observe.
Below, men and machines
choreograph destruction,
a ballet of bulldozers
and orchestrated trash—
compacting, covering,

pretending to cleanse.
The commissioner pauses,
surveying his domain of
transience: empire of ephemera
built on the bones of
yesterday's excess,

tomorrow's regret.
    In this dance of dirt and dust,
I find no rhythm but the
  persistent pulse of change,
the heartbeat of an earth
   that endures despite

our scarring hands.
A gull cries overhead,
its call a sharp contrast
to the muffled operations
below: nature's cry amid
the cacophony of the Anthropocene,

a piercing reminder of the wild.
     Here, where the land dips,
water gathers, reflecting
the broken sky, a mirror
to our fractured undertakings.

In this puddle, I see
the clouds frown back.
Leaves, displaced, swirl in
the wake of trucks,
   spiraling like lost desires,
caught in the eddy of

human whims and the
whirl of mechanical beasts.
The commissioner writes notes,
  his pen scratching a ledger
    of losses and gains,
a balance sheet of soil and soul,

calculating costs not counted,
in the currency of green.
He turns, a silhouette
against the encroaching dusk,
his outline blurring with the shadows
    of birds returning to roost—

the day ends, but the work,
  the reshaping, never ceases.
I wonder, as stars prick
the quickening dark,
about the stories we bury
beneath layers of loam and litter,

    what histories we write
   with the ink of our actions.
Night descends, and with it,
a cool silence settles over
  the churned earth: a blanket
to soothe the day's abrasions,

 a pause in the narrative
of ceaseless human toil.
The moon rises, indifferent,
casting pale light on
 the altered expanse:

beauty finds a place even
    in the disfigured landscapes,
casting shadows of hope.
Frost may soon lock
 this day's deeds beneath
its crystal quiet, preserving

this moment like an insect
in amber, frozen but
visible beneath the surface.
Yet, even as cold encases,
the earth beneath churns with
  latent life: worms navigate

  the netherworld, microbes
  break down the elements,
preparing for the spring.
This cycle of decay and growth,
mirrored in the heavens'
ceaseless cycles, reminds me:

   all is temporary under the
   great wheel of the sky,
    revolving, evolving, ever-turning.
under heavy treads, the land sighs:
its breath, a mist of dust and diesel,
and I stand: witness, rooted,

   observing nature's back, bent
   under the ambition of man:
this, a rhythm of relentless change.
dozers carve paths: arteries
that will never pulse,
cold steel against the warm earth,

pliant soil upturned, raw
and dark, wet with yesterday's
rain, glistening like a wound.
   how starkly we juxtapose,
this dance of metal and flesh,
    the commissioner points,

and a machine obeys:
it's a silent symphony
played on engines' roars.
ripples of debris migrate,
settling layers of history
one atop another: sediment

of consumption, fragments
of what was once whole,
all compiled in this new tomb.
bird shadows flit over chaos,
detached, ephemeral watchers,
a fleeting gesture against

the sprawl of our creation,
and I wonder if they mourn
the loss of their nesting ground.
the sky, too, feels closer,
heavy as if pressing down,
trying perhaps to reclaim

its stolen space, or maybe
to comfort the stripped earth,
offering gray clouds as a balm.
yet there's growth even here,
in the ugly scar of progress:
nature, resilient, sends up

shoots through fractured earth,
a defiant green against
the brown monochrome of upheaval.
in this upheaval, patterns emerge:
paths not taken, or perhaps

simply hidden beneath the rubble,
pointing toward an unknown,
as unpredictable as the flight
of ash in a fiery gust.
amidst the mechanical beasts,
a singular bloom dares to question,

its petal a testament to resilience,
to the enduring pulse beneath,
silent, yet screaming in color,
life asserting itself against odds.
the commissioner, distant figure,
moves through this tableau,

his steps inscribing authority
on the vulnerable earth,
his presence a sharp note
in the dirge of transformation.
each motion, each decision,
layers added, earth compacted,

a human-made ziggurat rising,
not to gods, but to consumption,
a temple to our enduring urge
to shape, control, redefine.
beneath it all, the deep hum,
not of machines, but of a heartbeat,

the slow, persistent drum
of earth's unyielding tempo,
resounding through the clamor,
reminding us: this is still a living thing.
waste becomes landscape,
landscape becomes myth,

in this new narrative we are
both destroyer and creator,
casting shadows long
as those of the circling birds.
but look how the shadows merge:

in the dim light, distinctions blur,
the bird, the waste, the earth,
all part of a grander dance of silhouettes,
each to their role, each to their part
in the relentless cycle of the seasons.
from above, the patterns show:

a patchwork quilt of use and reuse,
humankind's signature stitched
into the fabric of the planet,
a signature bold, perhaps impermanent,
fading like ink under the relentless sun.
in this moment of convergence,

the commissioner pauses,
as if hearing the subtle rhythms,
the whispered warnings of the soil,
his shadow cast long like a doubt,
or a question, left hanging in the dusk.
evening approaches subtly,

with the grace of the cooling air,
and dust settles slowly,
like memories, on the surfaces
of this newly shaped reality,
a veneer over the ancient skin of earth.
machines halt, one by one,

their engines' roar a final note
hanging in the cool evening,
and silence, that rare visitor,
finally descends, cloaking
the altered landscape in peace.

can peace truly inhabit this place?
or does it merely pause,
a fleeting visitor, like the birds,
or the light that plays
across the moved earth,
a brief, tender touch.

in the settling quiet,
thoughts turn like the earth,
pondering permanence,
the resilience of nature,
and our own fleeting imprint:
are we as enduring as we hope?

from the ruins, possibilities:
as the commissioner departs,
his vehicle stirring clouds of dust,
the scene reconfigures itself,
a canvas continuously painted
by the choices of those who wield the brush.

even now, the land whispers
of cycles, of storms yet to come,
of regrowth, and decay,
and rebirth, endlessly narrated
by the wind that carries seeds,
and dreams, across the reshaped plains.

will tomorrow recognize today?
or will it look upon this land
as a stranger, puzzled by
the scars we leave, the marks
of our passing, etched deep
in the narrative of the earth.

as machinery melds with dusk,
the commissioner's silhouette
grows fainter, blending into
the fabric of this transformed realm,
a mere character in the epic

of human ambition and nature's endurance.
the flap of wings, the distant hum,
all merge into a symphony,
the anthem of the Anthropocene,
a melody rich with contradiction,
sounding the depth of our impact,

echoing through the corridors of time.
what tales will these soils tell,
in the epochs that follow our own?
will they speak of wisdom, or of folly,
of the layers we've added,
the foundations we've shifted,

in our quest to sculpt the living earth?
underneath, the ancient hum persists,
a reminder that the beat goes on,
that what we perceive as permanence
is but a pause in the grand cadence,
a note held in the earth's vast chorus,

resounding with our temporary triumphs.
this tableau: stark, yet vibrant,
casts our shadows against
the vast backdrop of time,
where every action, every layer,

interacts in the dance of elements,
choreographed by forces beyond our ken.
as the last light fades,
as the machines cool,
as the commissioner vanishes
into the encroaching night,

the land holds its breath,
awaiting the next day's reshaping.
each dawn, a rebirth:
the continual recreation
of landscapes, both physical
and metaphysical, in the image

of our desires, our fears,
our indomitable will to change.
thus, the stage is set afresh,
each morning's light revealing
new angles, new challenges,
in the enduring drama of existence,

where we, fleeting as shadows,
seek to impose lasting impressions.
in endless cycles, we engage,
with the earth as our canvas,
our actions the strokes

that define, that refine,
    that ultimately intertwine
with the weft and warp of life.
each layer we add,
each decision we make,
shapes not just the landscape

but the legacy we leave,
the story told by the soil,
whispered by the wind,
sculpted by our collective hands.
as the sun sets on this scene,
the earth, resilient, prepares

for the night's cool embrace,
    and for the dawn that will surely follow,
  bringing light to our alterations,
and shadows to our ambitions.
in this interplay of light and dark,
of creation and destruction,

we find our place within the continuum,
molding the world as it molds us,
in an endless choreography
of relentless, rhythmic change.
Dust swirls up: machines groan,
their iron jaws clench soil,

rip through the calm of earth,
roots torn, unspoken spoils.
The Commissioner points,
gestures: a sweeping hand
over lands that once sprung wild,
    now obey a harsh command.

Thresholds of Adaptation

Edges of light bend,
each ray distorts:
I am the prism,
shattering unity
into spectra,
pulled apart.

Footfalls echo,
a soft patter on leaves:
each impact a drum,
signaling change,
resonate deep within,
my body speaks aloud.

Ribbons of shadow,
draw patterns on soil;
like veins under skin,
mapping routes unknown,
each a vital guide,
whispering paths.

Twilight deepens—
the edge of perception;
where clarity fades,
and mystery breathes,
enveloping me,
in its soft, gray coat.

This terrain varies,
subtle dips and rises;
like the beats of my heart,
irregular yet persistent,
defining life's rhythm,
against time's relentless march.

Knots in muscle,
mirrored in root and branch;
    interwoven struggles,
    the pain of growth,
strength born in tension,
binding tightly, releasing.

    Continuing on, I muse:
body's deviations,
not errors but scripts
for adaptation,
outlined by the fallen leaves,
mapped by the wandering ant.

Trees stand askew,
  witnesses to the wind's counsel;
    they sway, surviving,
lessons in resilience,
speaking strength,
in each bent bough.

    Sky now ink,
  stars pierce through;
points of reference
    in the vast, uncharted,
    illuminating the smallness,
our own perceived expanse.

  I ponder the webs,
from spider silk to neurons;
each connection vital,
each break consequential,
a network of infinite interactions,
    pulsing with shared destiny.

Breath visible in air,
coolness drawing out warmth;
contrasts define sensations,
teaching through opposites,
the necessity of differences,
to appreciate the whole.

Each step: a decision,
to engage with the uneven,
to learn the language,
of bumps and hollows,
nature's own morse code,
dotting the landscape.

Night's embrace tightens,
cool whisperings of dark;
though sight diminishes,
other senses heighten,
attuned to the nuances,
of a world obscured.

Footsteps meld with earth,
a gentle drum,
heartbeat of the terrain,
echoing my own,
in a symphony of steps,
composed by the journey.

Adaptation: a dance,
steps learned in the doing;
missteps, stumbles,
each a part of the choreography,
crafted by the necessity,
of movement, of survival.

A field, the stage,
   woods, the audience;
    I perform, unscripted,
under the scrutiny,
      of leafy canopies,
and critiqued by stars.

   Pause: to breathe,
inhale the scene;
each component,
a lesson in balance,
the art of standing,
despite the uneven ground.

   Continuing the stride,
     each movement deliberate;
aware of the shifts,
   the necessity of adjustment,
the body's quiet negotiations,
with the world it walks upon.

Each step: a testament,
to the power of adaptation;
how each misalign,
triggers a cascade of correction,
a silent, internal symphony,
played out in bones and sinew.

Sunset's last embers
flicker out beneath horizons;
darkness is not absence,
but a canvas for new thought,
where minds wander,
unfettered by the glare of day.

How easily a slip,
a mere twist of the foot,
alters the whole march,
the orchestrated normalcy,
revealing the fragility,
and resilience intertwined.

Contours of the path,
mold to my soles;
I shape it,
as it shapes me:
mutual crafting,
in each shared step.

What revelations,
do these simple adjustments hold?
In the micro-adjustments,
lie macro-cosmic truths,
the echo of my footfalls,
in the grand chamber of existence.

Stumble not just fault,
but opportunity,
to realign, reconsider,
the architecture of movement,
a chance to rebuild,
foundation stronger than before.

Night's curtain calls,
stars take their bows in the sky;
each light a story,
a distant echo of time,
inscribing their tales,
on the dark velvet above.

This journey in dimming light,
teaches more than sight could;
    in shadows, shapes form,
ideas manifest,
the unseen made visible,
through the lens of introspection.

Adapting: not just reaction,
  but also a creation,
a purposeful stride into unknown,
with the trust that each step,
   however uncertain,
leads towards understanding.

Physical shifts prompt,
mental reevaluations;
a recalibration of both,
body and mind,
navigating together,
the terrain of existence.

Nature's resilience,
a mentor in its silence;
  the trees' quiet dignity,
a lesson in standing,
despite the bends and twists,
life imposes.

Paths wind, as thoughts do,
each turn a new perspective;
   every angle offers
fresh vistas of understanding,
horizons expanded,
by the journey taken.

As night deepens,
the threshold appears;
between the physical walk,
and the mental journey,
each step a crossing,
from flesh to philosophy.

Here, in the quiet of evening,
under the watchful eyes of stars,
the question unfolds,
delicate as a fern frond;
what is adaptation,
but life's unending conversation?

A conversation,
between the world and the self,
a dialogue of adjustments,
each step a word,
each breath a sentence,
in the story we tell with our paths.

Long shadows cast,
by the sinking sun;
each one a dark brushstroke,
on the canvas of day,
drawing lines of connection,
between light and the lack thereof.

This interplay,
of light and shadow,
of body and thought,
weaves a tapestry,
rich with the hues,
of contemplation and experience.

As the landscape shifts,
so too does the mind;
each external change,
mirrors an internal one,
a reflection of the landscape,
in the contours of thought.

Twilight offers,
its lessons subtly;
under its transitory light,
truths shimmer briefly,
visible in the half-light,
where understanding deepens.

The path twists,
unexpected in its course;
each bend a mystery,
each straight a respite,
a rhythm found,
in the undulation of progress.

Nature's script, unwritten,
yet followed by all;
each creature, each plant,
adhering to roles unseen,
a performance perfected,
in the art of survival.

As night settles,
veiling the familiar,
the unknown becomes a friend,
its mystery a comfort,
in the promise of discovery,
with each uncertain step.

In this quietude,
the heart speaks louder;
its beats not just rhythms,
but echoes of a deeper connection,
to the pulse of the earth,
to the rhythm of the cosmos.

Twilight to night,
a symphony in shades;
each note played
on the spectrum of dusk,
a melody of colors,
fading into darkness.

Endings beckon new beginnings;
as light leaves, stars arrive,
each cycle a reminder,
of the infinite loops,
in which we spin,
participants in cosmic dances.

The quiet of the night,
a canvas for contemplation;
in silence, thoughts proliferate,
ideas germinate in the dark,
sprouting with the promise,
of dawn's nurturing light.

In this walk,
a microcosm of life;
each step a metaphor,
for broader journeys taken,
paths chosen,
in the forests of our lives.

The journey continues,
each step a narrative,
woven into the fabric,
  of the universe's vast tapestry,
a thread colored
by the hues of personal experience.

Here, amid the settling dusk,
lies a profound query,
held gently in the night's hands,
  open, unblinking:
what is the nature of adaptation,
and where do we find its threshold?

The earth, resilient:
taut as a drum, takes rest:
every hoof and heel,
    leaves its imprint: the weight
of lives in passage marked
by our step and stop.

Yet here, where twilight falls,
the shadows lean long and
crisp against the fading
  light, the day tapering
into a sliver of
soft dusk, tender and dim.

  Field boundaries blur, and
edges of the wild woods
embrace the open land:
    where I tread, a blend of
two worlds that speak of the
dualities within.

Limbs askew, carrying
burdens of altered gait,
whispers in each movement,
my body dialogues
quietly with itself:
an uneasy congress.

Muscles knot, pull, protest,
each step recalibrated,
a microcosm of
shift: how delicate this
balance, how easily
disturbed by a stray stone.

Trees stand testament to
the art of staying rooted
while reaching skyward: they,
like us, contend with their
own skew, twist, lean, and yet,
they rise, steadfast, undeterred.

The wind sifts through the leaves,
a hushing sound that seems
to soften the sharp edge
of my thoughts, mingling with
the scent of earth: a balm
for the restless spirit.

Isn't this the way of
all living things: adapting
to the light, the shadows,
to the winds that carve our
forms, to the rains that soothe
our parched, unspoken dreams?

Each adaptation a
silent transformation,
unnoticed until the
accumulation of
small shifts demands our
full, undivided gaze.

My body, a landscape
rich with the telltale signs
of time's relentless sculpt,
bears witness to the vast,
intricate interplay
of bone, sinew, and soul.

As the path curves, it takes
me along the boundary
where shadow integrates
with light, where each step is
both a question and a
declaration: I am.

Here, in the gentle close
of day, as night prepares
her deep embrace, I find
myself pondering the
thresholds crossed, the quiet
glimmers of transformation.

The resilience of bark,
the persistence of stem,
the surety of roots:
nature's lessons writ large
in the understory,
in the canopy's reach.

Temporal Sutures

I wake to a clock's march,
life spilling from each tick:
  as morning splits open,
its pages loose and sheer.
Days merge, ink to ink,
sutures of routine.

The potato steams, split:
a simple chord of joy
in chaos, routine's hug,
        dawn's early song bursts,
    before light claims the blue,
life's small, sweet echo.

  Breaths in the broth of now,
  acts tiny yet profound,
whispers of past and next,
ditches from rain's stay,
  mere trickles mirroring
      my split joy and despair.

On edges of deep known,
peering into the self,
the chasm asks of us
not who, but what we are:
soul's landscape ever shifts,
under the vast skies' play.

Even as forms change,
  life's ambiguity,
terrifying, mesmerizes.
Each spark lights, then dims,
  paths illuminated,
then dark once again.

Yet, a wriggle persists,
a light whispering resilience,
not in clear phrases but
through being's sheer pulse,
where all life shares a tongue:
survival, adaptation, yield.

Brief custodians we are,
of moments not our own,
part of stretches unseen,
beyond our simple grasp,
where life's dance evades,
delicate, yet never held.

Morning comes again,
its relentless ticking loud,
yet within, a calm brews
as if chaos could teach
the pace of still waters,
and the calm of deep seas.

Each tick a question,
each tock an answer,
life's endless dialogue
with itself, with the void,
balancing on fine threads
spun from dawn's first light.

How formless the thought,
how structured the heart,
pulsing with the rhythms
of days, of years, of life,
each beat a narrative
in the cosmos's vast book.

Where yesterday bleeds
into tomorrow's void,
  there, in the overlap,
      finds our truest selves,
not in the distinct days
but blended, as one stream.

  Potatoes, buttered, split:
  so mundane, yet so vast,
a universe within skins,
worlds held in steam's rise,
each molecule a story,
unfolding with the heat.

     And so it is with us,
  particles of vast plays,
    acting out scripts written
by the stars, by the dust,
    by the hands of time
shaping the clay of souls.

Each morning, a layer,
    unfurls like fresh ink
    on a page never read,
every day a new verse
  in the poem of a lifetime,
written but unread.

In the simple, the complex,
in the quiet, a loud echo,
the universe speaks soft,
in the spread of dawn,
     in the curl of steam,
where all stories merge.

Continuity and change,
joy shadowed by despair,
across the breadth of life,
we stand, we falter,
forever on the brink,
ever on the cusp.

Mirrors in trickles,
reflections in streams,
what is seen is partial,
the unseen vast and deep,
as if every reflection
hints at more unseen.

The chasms within us
ask not who, but what,
as nature queries softly,
do you see what you are?
Not just the surface
but the depths untold.

This landscape of souls,
ever morphing, shifting,
like earth beneath skies,
terrifying yet mesmerizing,
each moment a spark,
each second a flame.

Amid existential paths,
small lights guide subtly,
whispering of resilience,
in cryptic tongues of life,
not words but existences,
where we all speak survival.

Custodians of moments,
passengers on journeys,
stretching far beyond
  our own horizons,
where mysteries dance,
    just out of reach.

Between tangible and fathom,
  the dance of life plays,
balancing on threads,
woven by the cosmos,
  where each step we take
  is part of a greater ballet.

    Yet, as day claims night,
and light shadows dark,
we find in each transition,
a mirror of our own,
reflecting the dualities
that carve our very souls.

In the silence of growth,
  in the noise of decay,
  find the essence of being,
the core of existence,
    not in loud declarations,
    but in quiet revelations.

   Morning's relentless tick,
    a backdrop to thoughts,
each unfurling like pages,
    as unread books await,
   their stories untold,
     their meanings layered.

Steam rises, simple truths:
echoes of warmth and need,
as butter melts into flesh,
fusing with earth's yields,
showing how even small
acts are ties to the vast.

Continuity in the dawn chorus,
change in the sky's hues,
interconnected in breaths,
woven by threads unseen,
each bird's call, each light shift,
a part of the cosmic loom.

So the days stack,
each upon the other,
a staircase to somewhere,
or perhaps nowhere at all,
each step a story,
each story a step.

The relentless ticking,
yet a comforting beat,
like the heart's own drum,
echoing through the chambers
of days, of years, of lives,
all connected, all apart.

Buttered bread, steaming tea,
simple pleasures, small joys,
amid the vast chaos of being,
anchors in the flow of time,
reminders of the constancy,
the continuity of small acts.

Each morning, a fresh page,
each night, a closed book,
in the library of existence,
  where every book waits,
its spine stiff with potential,
its pages eager to turn.

  And as the potato cools,
and the steam dissipates,
  so too do our moments,
each cooling into memory,
each memory a layer,
   in the sediment of self.

These moments:
     a continuity,
connected by the filament
    of hours and dreams,
unraveling gently: yet,

     each tick a robust beat,
    within the clock's steady march,
each click a reminder:
life is not stationary,
    but a progression,
a climb, a growth,

inward, outward, upward:
the potato steams, opens,
      the earth turns, exposes
its myriad faces to us,
     and the dawn chorus sings:
      a celebration of the new,

each note a delicate thread
    in the fabric of the morning,
  weaving sound with light:
patterns emerge,
the texture of life,
      intertwined like tree roots,

seeking sustenance, sharing
a soil, fed by past falls,
and rains that wrote
their own stories,
  pooled in the impressions
left by yesterday's boots,

reflecting today's sky,
a mirror, a pause,
    to ponder the depth:
how deep do these waters go?
    how many reflections
  before we see beneath?

skin of the surface:
  trembling with every breeze,
each ripple a reaction,
   a response to the winds
     that dance with fate,
as they whisper through leaves,

those green tongues,
repeating secrets of old,
encoded in chlorophyll,
  under the sun's interrogation,
the plot thickens,
  as roots delve deeper:

is this not a type of reading?
  the soil's nutrients, a script,
  the plant's growth, an interpretation,
a translation of elements,
      from earth to air,
carbon to oxygen,

    the simple alchemy
    of survival, effortless,
yet profound in its simplicity,
a potato on a plate,
   a tree stretching skyward,
both alive, exchanging

with their environments,
in silence, yet eloquently:
their existence a statement,
a contribution to the dialogue
between species, generations,
a shared journey on this sphere,

a sphere suspended in velvet,
the cosmos, indifferent or watchful,
  each star a witness,
each planet a participant,
in the dance of orbits,
a slow waltz,

across millennia,
each step measured,
each turn a calculation,
by the grand choreographer,
a universe unfolding,
      each galaxy a flourish,

each nebula a breath drawn,
in the vast lungs of space,
where time dilates,
and we find ourselves here,
microcosms,
mimicking the macro,

our cells, our societies,
complex, each cosmos,
each thought, each action,
ripples in the pond of being,
each decision a divergence,
the paths we walk,

branches in the fractal forest,
a forest where light breaks,
softly, through leaves,
casting patterns on the ground,
each dapple a pixel,
of the larger image we're part of,

a picture we paint daily,
with actions, words, silences,
each color chosen carefully,
or sometimes recklessly,
in the art of living,
art, science, philosophy—

blurred lines in the sand,
the tide washes over,
and we draw anew,
seeking only to understand,
understand the cycles,
the rhythms, the phases,

the phases of the moon,
the tides she governs,
the pull she exercises,
over oceans, over beings,
over the sap that flows,
silent yet palpable,

a force unseen but felt,
a gravitational poetry,
poetry in the mundane,
the ordinary: a potato,
steaming, the sunset,
a daily disappearance,

spectacular in its ordinariness,
and we, attendees,
at the show of shows,
where the curtain never falls,
but constantly reveals
new acts, unexpected twists,

twists in our paths,
our personal plotlines,
where characters enter,
and exit, each leaving
a mark, a lesson,
Morning splits: light anew,

its glow, a soft deluge,
spreading thin over leaf,
over stem: the dew finds
paths unseen, moves in swift
silence, marking its course.
Daylight weaves through branches,

threads gold in the canopy:
      each leaf, a mirror of
the sun's ascent, reflects
  the transition from dark
to a bright, bold expanse.
The morning, routine yet

renewed, stitches itself
   into the fabric of
the vast, eternal sky:
      an infinite canvas,
painted daily by time.
With each dawn, I wonder,

    am I the same being
that greeted yesterday's
    first light, or have I changed,
molten, reshaped by the
incessant flow of life?
      As roots cling to the earth,

steadfast through storms and still
    in calm, so does the core
of my being hold tight
to what seems immutable,
unchanged amid chaos.
Yet, beneath this stillness,

a turmoil: thoughts like leaves
in a storm, swirling, lost
    to the whirlwind of self—
a dance of existence,
chaotic, yet precise.

Cycles of Defiance

Stretching limbs, the old tree
waits: a testament to time,
years scored in skin's deep wrinkles,
roots clutching earth, holding firm,
  yet yearning skyward.
Leaves, a fresh green shock,

dare to whisper: resist the fall,
a cycle's new defiance,
speaking growth amidst decay,
      life's pulse in dying light.
Third leaves trace the air,
patterns unseen but felt,

   each lift and dip a story,
penned in chlorophyll,
      and light, and shadow.
Their veins like rivers map,
a coursing life force flows,
from stem to stern, channeling

essence, like blood in veins,
each leaf alive with potential.
Thus stands the gnarled guardian,
a girth of ages wide,
  drawing from the sun's warmth,
    yet shading the sod below,

a dance of give and take.
   Life's symphony plays in whispers,
rustling through treetop and bough,
notes high and low, mingled,
a canopy's quiet concerto,
unfolding in green waves.

Mortality, like a shadow, creeps,
subtly, it dims the day,
yet in this soft encroaching,
wisdom finds its fertile ground,
sprouting, even in twilight's chill.
A tree, like man, contemplates,

its own inevitable wilt,
branches heavy with the past,
yet new shoots strive, reaching out,
defying the quietus.
Do leaves dream of being buds?
Or cherish their fleeting flare,

in the grand, orchestrated
collapse into nutrient earth,
recycled, reborn, restored?
Each leaf a fluttering heart,
each drop of dew, a tear,
shed in the knowing of ends,

yet celebrating the cycle,
a flourish in the face of night.
So cycles spin, relentless,
the tree observes, endures,
part of a larger weave,
threads pulling, tugging,

in the fabric of existence.
Beneath bark, a slow pulse thrums,
sap's sweet course through hidden veins,
a slow dance of sugars and sunlight,
photosynthesizing life,
an alchemy of air and earth.

Even as shadows lengthen,
under the boughs, life teems,
moss carpets the ancient roots,
insects burrow, birds nest,
a community thrives in decline.
Yet, does the tree lament?

Or does it accept each phase,
from verdant youth to brittle bone,
as part of its destined arc,
scripted by time's unyielding hand?
Roots, like memories, delve deep,
touching stones, soaked in lore,

drawing sustenance from stories,
from layers of life compressed,
feeding today with yesterday's tales.
And so stands the ancient one,
a beacon, a bastion, a bridge,
between what was, what is,

what passes and what persists,
seasoned yet ever sprouting anew.
In every leaf, a lesson,
in every ring, a record,
history held in hardwood,
silent but for the whisper,

when wind wanders through.
Old age and new growth duel,
intersecting in layered barks,
a quiet battlefield, where
life and death negotiate,
each claiming victory in turns.

Thus, the cycle turns,
the elderly tree, like aged men,
    hosts a riotous revival of leaves,
mocking the steady hand of decline
with bursts of unexpected life.
   Amid such cycles, selves spin,

the pull of dimming dreams,
against the bright burst of now,
a leaf unfurls, fragile yet fierce,
in the face of the falling dusk.
      The stark reality breathes cold,
     yet within it, potential warms,

the whale of awareness leaps,
from denial's deep waters,
  embracing the chill of the air.
Confronting the end, yet not ending,
striving, not merely surviving,
     finding form in the formless,

tracing trajectories unseen,
in the interstices of existence.
     Rooted, yet reaching, a life
unfolds in layered complexity,
   from core to skin, from seed to sky,
in the enduring dance of days,

where each moment matters.
The philosophy of existence,
woven through with the threads,
of cosmic energy, mundane
and magnificent, minute
and massive, melding into myth.

Every jest, every earnest tone,
Grapples with the essence of being,
seeking meaning in action
and reaction, the spirals
and stalls of life's wide web.
In simple observation:

the motions of existence,
the core of wisdom found,
morality in movement,
each deliberate, each delayed.
And so, the ancient tree stands,
witnessing, withering, yet willing,

new leaves against old wood,
a testament to the persistent
pull of life, against the gravity of time.
Deep in the ground, roots
grasp at ancient soils:
they pull, they coil around

nutrients, water, stories
long gone into the silent
earth—carbon cycles, slow.
Branches stretch, wry smiles
against a gray sky: they
do not know the end,

nor contemplate
their leafy bursts
as omens, just cycle.
Photosynthesis—golden
alchemy turning light
into life: veins channel

sun's radiant offering
to cores where sap
tangos with bark, flush.
Leaves unfurl, late,
    like old hands—wrinkled,
yet grasping anew at the

frayed edges of youth,
mockery, perhaps, or defiance
in the face of twilight's sigh.
Cycles spiral: birth, bloom,
decay—philosophical
in their indifference,

    yet charged with
the same cosmic dust
    that dreams are spun from.
Petals witness, fall—
the inevitable drift
towards sleep, towards

that darker soil where
all must lay their head
and reckon with roots.
Still, the old tree—
its sap, a sticky residue
    of years, it beats with

a persistence: heartwood
echoing the songs
of a stubborn sunrise.
Here is life, flickering,
bright as a comet's
  tail, burning not

out of despair but out
of sheer will to
engrave light onto the dark.
I watch the leaves,
their audacious green
is a testament—not

of naiveté, but of
a seasoned bravery,
a willingness to dance again.
Nature, ever fluent
in the art of renewal,
whispers secrets:

one must lean
in close, listen
beneath the rustle.
The tree, like me,
bears the scars,
the rings deep

within its core:
each a story, a year,
a burst of life or sorrow.
The sun sets, reddish,
painting an end that
seems too sweet, too

gentle for the finality
it brings with each
day's quiet death.
Night embraces canopy,
each leaf a somber
note in the dark symphony—

yet, within this natural
  repose, lies the seed
of another day's rise.
  Roots delve deeper,
as if to anchor the
passing time,

holding tight to
what earth offers:
  stability, memory, life.
The cycle turns,
  a wheel upon which
all ride unknowingly,

destined to follow
the arc from zenith
    to horizon's gentle dip.
And so, it spins—
each turn a narration
of beginnings, peaks,

falls, and the quiet
ebb that speaks
of rest, of endings.
Embracing the silence,
the tree finds peace
in its stature, its reach

towards the stars—
branches like fingers
    poised in final benediction.
  Yet, within the quiet,
a small shoot emerges—
  unexpected green

against the bark's
time-etched gray;
life persists, insists.
This dance, this interplay
between life and the ever
nearing whisper of

nonexistence, crafts
a delicate balance,
a harmony profound.
We witness, partake—
each of us a leaf, a branch,
a trunk rooted in our

own landscapes, our
existence equally
fraught with cycles.
The philosophical bend,
the look inward and
outward simultaneous,

offers no easy peace,
but a dynamic, ever
evolving understanding.
Thus, in the decay—
in the falling leaves,
the bare branches,

there lies an inherent
sweetness, a decay
not of ends but beginnings.
Threads of mortality,
woven seamlessly
into the fabric of

our daily lives, remind
us: we are part of
this grand, unending weave.
As I stand, tree-like,
pondering the flux
of my own seasons,

I find solace in the
natural order, the
inevitable patterns of existence.
Through observation,
through the patient
watching of life's

simple, yet profound
motions, wisdom
slowly unfurls its quiet power.
Actions, reactions—
the narrative spells itself
across the landscape

in deliberate pulses,
each movement a
story, each tale a life.
The cycle continues,
as it must, as it always
has—each ending an

echo of a beginning,
each beginning a soft
whisper of an ending.
Here, under the old tree,
I grasp at the lessons—
like roots searching

in the dark for water,
I seek nourishment
in life's enduring dance.
Nature's script,
written in the spirals
of seeds, the branching

of neurons, speaks
of interconnections
deep, vast, essential.
In this dialogue,
between the light
and dark, the seen

and unseen, lies
the true essence
of being, of existing.
Thus, we move—
each of us an actor
upon this verdant stage,

each playing out
our roles within the
wider cosmic story.
And in these moments—
these flashes of green
among the graying,

we find not just
a defiance of age,
but a celebration of life.
As the cool winds
usher in the night's
deepening shadow,

we, like the old tree,
stand firm, roots
intertwined with time.
The journey is both
individual and shared,
a path trodden alone,

yet accompanied by
every leaf, every branch,
every whispering breeze.
In the quiet, the profound,
in the simple observation
of life's enduring cycle,

we discover not just the
nature of our days,
but the daylight within ourselves.
The roots I know: deep, entwined,
beneath soil's dark embrace:
but at the tip, a fresh green,

unexpected, almost brazen:
this burst: this late-life rising:
how odd it feels, this newness.
In youth, plans shot like stars,
endlessly bright and point-bound:
now, those paths seem blurred,

edges softened by time's wear:
yet here, this sharp green,
spiteful against the fade.
Is it defiance, this late sprout?
or merely life, unyielding,
resisting the narrative of decline.

Cycle's Witness

In this space, the twilight:
garden shadows lengthen,
drawing cold from the sun's
last warmth: the cycle
renews again: nature's
delicate rhythm pulses.

Yet, amidst this calm,
the tabby stirs, muscles
  taut, amber eyes locked
    on movement: a dance
of life and death begins:
      ground rules, unwritten.

A whisper of leaves,
      the chipmunk, unaware,
nibbles at fallen seeds:
tiny heartbeat a drum
     of innocence: nature's
child, unversed in fear.

With a silent approach,
    precision of the wild,
      tabby inches closer:
each step calculated,
a soft paw on dew grass,
a breath held in time.

     The standoff is brief:
movements quicksilver—
dissonant yet aligned:
survivor’s strategy,
evolution's playbook
  etched in each sinew.

Rushed escape, chipmunk
darts—a blur of brown
and fear: a near miss,
yet the cycle holds true:
death's shadow passes:
life breathes, for now.

Moments like these,
small yet profound,
echo the larger frame
of existence: I watch,
drawn into the weave

of the immediate world.
There's a simplicity
in these interactions
that belies the complex
nature of being: life,
a network of narratives

entangled in survival.
Each creature plays
a part scripted long
before its breath:
hunter or hunted,
each role necessary,

balancing the scales.
The tabby, though failed,
slips away, dignity intact,
essence of predator dimmed
by hunger not sated:
a stoic acceptance of

the role it must perform.
In my reflection, I see
how all lives intertwine:
my presence just another
layer in this tapestry
of existence: observer

and participant alike.
Thoughts turn inward:
how often do we see
our own survival mirrored
in such honest displays?
We hunt, and are hunted,

in myriad metaphorical ways.
Yet, this pure moment
offers a rare clarity:
life, in its raw essence,
demands not just action
but contemplation: to see

beyond the surface fray.
So, as the garden settles,
night's curtain drawing near,
I reflect on the tabby,
the chipmunk, the dance
of life and escape: lessons

beneath the evening stars.
Each creature's breath,
a note in the symphony
of existence: all connected,
each dependent on the
balance of this delicate,

incessant rhythm.
And as the stars appear,
illuminating the garden,
their ancient light whispers
of larger forces at play:
a universe of interactions,

endless, profound.
I stand, a solitary figure,
caught in the web of life,
each movement a part
of something greater:
a participant in the

sacred cycle of being.
The garden, now quiet,
holds the stories of the night:
predator and prey,
the watched and the watcher,
all woven into the fabric

of this cosmic play.
In the stillness, I ponder
the roles we inhabit,
the lines we recite:
do we truly understand
our place on this stage,

or do we merely play along?
The cycle continues,
unbroken, as the garden
breathes under starlight:
each creature, each life,
a thread in the tapestry

that is existence.
And so, with a quiet heart,
I watch, and learn,
and wonder at this simple truth:
that to be alive is to be
a part of something vast,

beautiful, and terrifying.
As I turn to leave,
the garden whispers,
a soft reminder of
the dance that never ends:
life and death,

predator and prey.
In the gentle wash of dawn,
the garden hums its old song,
the yellow tabby, still, waits:
her whiskers twitch, the dance
of predator and prey begins,

momentarily entrenched.
Her eyes, twin moons of focus,
gaze upon the unsuspecting flutter,
Chipmunk, little harbinger
of life's fragile thread, scouts
for morsels among fallen leaves,

unknowingly casting its fate.
This sacred theater plays out,
unscripted: the rustling leaves,
silent witnesses to the hunt,
whisper tales of survival,
where even the predator

knows hunger's sharp bite.
The stalk: careful, deliberate,
each muscle tuned to silence,
  a natural orchestration:
She moves, a shadow's breath,
cloaked by the dawn's soft light,

a specter in the garden's heart.
The chase, sudden and fierce,
ignites: all nature holds its breath
  as destiny unfurls in leaps
and bounds—life's pulse quickened
by the necessity of the moment,

    the unyielding decree of hunger.
But the rabbit, quick and lithe,
flirts with fate and bounds away,
  its heartbeat a drum, rapid
against the quiet morning air,
   echoing the ancient rhythm

  of escaped prey and thwarted hunter.
The tabby, undeterred, resumes her post,
  tail flicking with contemplation,
   pondering the almost was,
the near capture of breath
and body—nature's gamble laid

bare on the loam's dark canvas.
Her golden coat blends back
into the tapestry of the dawn,
  each thread a narrative, woven
    with the fine sinews of survival,
the ceaseless cycle of life, death,

and the pursuit nestled between.
   The air vibrates with the song
of those who evade and those who yearn,
an endless loop that binds
each to the other in mutual need,
    a delicate balance: the rhythm

of existence, a heartbeat shared.
   One life flutters, another paces,
   each caught in the script written
by unseen hands, in ink of dew
      and the blood of the fallen,
a story retold each day,

under the watchful gaze of dawn.
The chipmunk, unaware of its part,
scurries, a tiny heart fueled
by sun and shadow, unaware
of the eyes that follow each move,
a miniature ballet played

      on the stage of the earth.
It pauses, senses the shift,
the subtle change in the air,
the narrative's twist, unknowable,
      yet felt in the tremor of leaves,
the sudden silence that falls

like a verdict from the sky.
Silhouette against the breaking day,
   the tabby crouches, calculating,
a geometry of motion and intent,
each muscle coiled, each thought
aligned with the primal textbook—

lessons written in sinew and instinct.
So unfolds the day's lesson,
etched in the quiet theater of nature,
where each actor knows their cue,
their entrance and exit marked
by the sun's steady arc, their roles

defined by the hunger they carry.
Line is drawn, cycle spins,
in the garden's heart, life whispers:
    of prey and predator, of survival,
each chapter closes only to open anew,
     bound by the eternal rhythm,

the pulse of the living earth.
  And as the sun climbs, the scene fades,
the players retreat, their stories
tucked beneath wings and whispers,
the garden—a stage emptied,
saving its tales for the morrow,

under the watchful stars' dim glow.
The dew, a silver lining,
clings to each grass blade:
a fragile network,
    echoing wider cosmos.

Here, where earth meets sky,
a field of tensions plays.
The yellow tabby waits,
      pauses: muscles taut,
its amber eyes, twin moons,
reflecting a primal knowledge,

the patience: layered deep,
within its sinew and bone.
In the underbrush, rustle,
a small heart quickens,
chipmunk, small and lithe,
skitters near the fence line,

aware of shadows shifting,
overhead and all around.
Life pulses, uncompromising,
each actor set in motion:
predator and the prey,
enacting ancient scripts,

woven into their essence,
stitched into the landscape.
Sun filters through branches,
creating mosaics of light,
the dance of leaves shadows:
a delicate ballet of quiet,

disrupted by sudden movement,
a quickening in the air.
The chase ensues: swift,
unyielding as gravity's pull,
the tabby's body: a fluid line,
melding speed with silence,

while the chipmunk darts—
hope, a whisper, fleeting.
A miss: the air cuts empty,
and life, by a thread, hangs,
the rabbit's leap: a salvation,
ephemeral against the morning,

where survival writes itself,
in lines sharp and thin.
Yet, in this swift exchange,
    a drama subtle unfolds,
reflecting broader circles—
life, death, interwoven,

like roots beneath the soil,
that support and strangle.
The yellow tabby turns,
its journey not in vain,
  the hunt a meditation,
on nature's simple truths:

    existence is a balance,
  harsh, yet profoundly fair.
 The garden breathes a sigh,
life trembles on the brink,
each creature plays its part,
in this eternal, delicate,

dance of shadows and light,
 each life a note in the symphony.
Under the pink-tinted sky,
the chipmunk pauses: free,
its survival not mere chance,
but a piece of the puzzle,

that is larger than itself,
echoing in the cool air.
As the garden's heart beats,
  in rhythms soft and clear,
    the tabby cleans its whiskers,
and somewhere in the brush,

a tiny heartbeat slows,
savoring the dawn's caress.
Each moment here, a microcosm,
reflects a universe beyond,
where predator and prey find,
their places in the script,

written long before they tread,
this small stage of earth and green.
The garden, a classroom,
where lessons hard are learned,
and taught by nature's hand,
unyielding, yet it gives,

teaching us to watch, to see,
not just look, at life's woven tapestry.
We, observers on the fringe,
see the dance of survival,
a tableau rich and deep,
where lives are lost and found,

and the value of each breath,
is measured in silent beats.
So in this brisk morning air,
where dew still glistens clear,
I find a truth simple and stark:
the beauty of living is not,

just in surviving the dark,
but in savoring the light.
And as the day unfolds,
the garden does not forget,
those players small and large,
who've danced their parts well,

under the sky’s watchful eye,
recording each leaf and cry.
Thus, as I stand and watch,
the lessons of nature unfold,
the threads of life and death,
tangled in a dance divine,

revealing to those who see,
the beauty in survival's line.
The yellow tabby stretches,
under the now high sun,
its day of hunt concluded,
win or lose, life goes on,

in this small patch of earth,
that mirrors the world beyond.
In every leaf or drop of dew,
in every chase or quiet wait,
there lies a story to be told,
of a life, a death, a fate,

in the garden’s humble stage,
where nature dictates the play.
And as I leave the morning,
to go about my day,
the garden's lessons linger,
in my mind, they play and sway,

teaching me the rhythms,
of life, in its raw array.
Thus we live, thus we watch,
each day a new performance,
where simple truths are taught,
under the guise of ordinary.

Shifting Winds

Winds shift: the day begins
  with sunlight spilling
over dew-laden grass:
each drop reflects
  a microcosm: boundless,
within its gleaming edge.

Leaves whisper ancient
secrets: how cycles
spin: endless:
root to tip to fall:
return: the soil beckons,
      life anew from death's call.

Breezes carry pollen,
    tiny helmsman steering
through the vast skies:
their journey set
by unseen currents,
paths entwined, artfully met.

Birds trace arcs,
pure in their simplicity:
  each wingbeat
a stroke against
the canvas of the morning,
painting choruses that linger.

Rivers, too, tell tales
as they carve the earth:
  water meeting stone—
      resistance: a conversation
    between hard and soft:
molded by persistence.

Roots delve deep,
grasping: not just soil,
but the heart of existence:
connected below, unseen,
aiding each other in silence:
a subterranean alliance.

Mountains loom,
silent sentinels of epochs,
their rocky faces:
scarred by time,
weathered yet unwavering,

holding centuries within.
Glaciers creep,
slowly sculpting valleys,
their icy touch:
a harsh mentor
to landscapes, teaching

the art of slow change.
Stars, distant yet present,
navigate our nights:
each a beacon,
ancient and precise,
guiding wayfarers

beneath their silent watch.
Moons wax and wane,
their phases a dance
of shadow and light:
quietly influencing
tides and creatures,

in rhythms long understood.
Atoms buzz relentlessly,
bound by forces
meticulously precise:
a ballet on a microscopic
stage: unseen yet

integral to all forms.
Cells divide, lives weave,
each existence linked
by invisible threads:
a tapestry vast and varied,
each thread a story,

each story a beginning.
Life pulses, ebbs, flows,
mirroring the cycles
found in larger frames:
seasons change:

the same yet ever different,
each turn a fresh rendition.
Leaves die and fall,
their colors a final flourish
before returning to the earth:
composition decomposes,

feeding the next cycle,
a perpetual renewal.
Seeds settle into dark,
the cold earth embracing
potential: silent, waiting,
for warmth's return:

trigger of life's symphony,
played anew each year.
  Insects flit through air,
delicate yet determined:
    survival in each flutter,
each a small cog

  in the broader mechanism
of ecosystem intricacies.
Clouds form, disperse:
vapors gathered then freed,
painting skies with
the artistry of the transient:

each shape a story,
dissolved by wind's whims.
Rains come, bearing
life's quintessence:
    each drop a carrier
of change, a sculptor

of landscapes,
nourisher of thirsts.
   Soil, rich and fragrant,
cradles seeds, feeds roots:
a foundation laid

beneath our feet,
quietly critical
in life's grand opera.
Sunsets, daily finales
stunning in their brevity,
paint the horizon

with fleeting mastery,
endings that promise
tomorrow's fresh canvas.
Stars again appear,
ushers of the night,
each twinkle a reminder:

the vastness above mirrors
the vastness within,
boundless potential.
Night deepens, cradling
the world in its dark arms,
a blanket under which

all life pauses,
breaths syncing
with the slow pulse of dark.
Dreams weave through sleep,
consciousness in freefall,
tumbling through memories,

hopes, fears: mingled
in the quiet theatre
of the resting mind.
Morning returns,
with its gentle light:
a soft nudge,

a whisper to awaken,
to rise and begin again:
life's tender insistence.
Through days and nights,
seasons and cycles,

life dances: poised
between starts and ends,
each moment a step,
each step a story.
Amidst the folds of shadowed light,
each leaf a crisp, silvery note,

nature sings through brisk air:
we are but whispers in the vast,
the silence and the echo intertwined,
a breath at dawn, subtle yet profound.
The rhythms of the earth pulse,
silent thrums below our feet,

roots delve deep, reaching out
to the secrets kept by the cold soil,
each microbe stirring, a universe below,
binding the seen to the unseen.
The chill wind narrates a tale,
of beginnings scrubbed into endings,

the frost, its etchings intricate,
a script of survival, a test,
coded deep within the dance
of decay and renewal, cycle spun.
Who are we but observers,
tracing lines that stars etch

in the fabric of dark,
each point a reflection
of distances unreachable,
yet felt within the pulse of the heart?
Galactic dust, our primal kin,
mingles with the breath of pines,

the mountains wear their snowy caps,
guardians of the high, thin air,
where thoughts clear as daylight,
sharpening perspective, a keen blade.
Entropy, a truth relentless,
spins its threads through all,

the chaos a disguised order,
complex, as the fractal frost,
where every end's a shaky start,
a murmur in the symphony of the void.
The river meanders, a silver path,
its waters a mirror to the sky,

reflecting the cosmos' quiet gaze,
does it know the ocean's depth,
or the storm's fleeting fury?
It flows, aware only of its flowing.
Beneath the bark, the tree holds stories,
rings mark time in silent speech,

each layer a testament to seasons past,
witness to the storms endured,
growth amidst the trials,
the branching paths of fate.
In this woven mesh, our lives
intersect with the flutter of leaves,

the migrations of clouds overhead,
patterns recognized, a comfort,
in their predictable unpredictability,
a paradox embraced.
The philosopher ponders the tree,
not for fruit or shade,

but for the essence of treeness,
in the curve of its bough,
   the spread of its silent roots,
an understanding, fundamental, yet fleet.
Our musings, too, are seeds,
      cast by the winds of contemplation,

taking root in terrains unseen,
do they find soil or stone?
It matters not: the act of seeking
is itself a form of finding.
In the flicker of day's end,
the light bends into shadows:

each curve a tale of time
    and the bending, a path
to unknown descents,
connecting us.
The sky, a vast canvas
stroked by the hues

  of falling night, whispers
of transitions so gentle,
as if to imply the ease
in which day succumbs.
Life's pulsing ceaselessly,
through veins of leaves

and the vast arteries
of wind-carved canyons,
teaches of continuance,
the pulse within stasis.
A leaf detaches, aloft,
hovering past its tree:

not apart, but a phase
of an ever-extended breath,
returning to the soil
    to nourish anew.
In the soil, a microcosm,
busy with decay and birth:

atoms exchanged in
  silent bartering,
offer the blueprint
of boundlessness.
  Roots delve deeper,
stretching through earth,

grasping the essence
    of moistened minerals,
  drawing sustenance
from the quiet dark.
Above, stars ignite
in the clear night's veil,

  their cold fire mirroring
the sparks within us;
each a reminder of
our contained infinity.
    The horizon blurs,
where earth meets sky,

    echoing the edges
of our understanding,
where knowing melds
into feeling.
    Molecules dance
in the spaces between,

the intimacy of atoms
unseen yet profound,
like the thoughts that
thread through minds.
A river carves its bed,
not merely eroding but

shaping a path for flow:
so too do our choices
sculpt the landscapes
of our fates.
Creeks murmur secrets,
in a language pristine,

to rocks, roots, and reeds:
listen, they counsel softly,
there's wisdom in the
water's way.
As the moon ascends,
its serene light casting

shadows of the known,
we perceive the cycles
that guide us,
inevitable as tides.
Beneath this moon,
a sapling shivers, its

tender form basking
in the glow of growth,
each leaf a small ode
to the cosmos.
Seasons shift subtly,
a slow painting over

of landscapes familiar,
each stroke a note
in a symphony of
constant change.
Cold seeps gently,
nudging the warmth away,

in its place, a crispness
that awakens the skin,
reminding us of the
cycles within cycles.
Frost patterns on glass,
each crystal a masterpiece,

brief and destined to melt,
reflect the transient art
of our own paths,
etched and erased.
Breath visible in chill air,
a cloud of life's rhythm,

exhaling worries,
inhaling moments
fresh with the scent
of possibilities.
In the seamless shift
from night to dawn,

a silence profound
carries the weight
of beginnings, pregnant
with the day's promise.
Thus we stand,
at the precipice of cycles,

watching the play
of light and shadow,
knowing in each end,
a beginning murmurs.
How like the mountain and air,
our thoughts mingle,

ideas taking flight on
winds of contemplation,
soaring high, yet
rooted deeply.
From the peak's solitude,
the view sprawls vast:

a tapestry woven with
the threads of lives
intersecting, parting,
a dance of destinies.
Such is the nature of this
journey, encircling back,

where every ending point
meets its start,
in the quiet assurance
of the looping path.
Navigating this terrain,
with compass points

set in the heart and mind,
steering through fog
and clear, the same,
guided by inner stars.
Reversals turn to advances,
as we learn the steps.

Market's Pulse

Through rows of color:
peaches blush in morning's kiss,
tomatoes glint: red jewels,
herbs breathe out their lively zest,
wood creaks: stalls under weight,
and cloths flutter like soft wings.

Hands reach: old rhythms,
new spices mix with legacy,
leathery faces crease in sun,
smiles: seasoned, deepened,
eyes bright as they survey,
baskets filled with yester's toil.

Lake breezes mingle:
scent of fish blends with basil,
voices rise and fall: waves,
each syllable a pebble
tossed in the vast lake of air,
rippling out to silent edges.

He stands: back bowed,
not with burden but time,
crutches tap-dance on stone,
each step a testament,
to years worn proudly,
like medals from unseen wars.

She moves among the stalls,
more slowly than last June,
her body a diary of seasons,
her hands glide over fabric,
touching not just cloth but,
the hands that weaved them.

Children dash: laughter sprouts,
quick as the darting dragonflies,
they weave through legs and baskets,
a reminder of cycles spinning,
infinite as the lake's embrace,
brief as the spark in their eyes.

Conversations blossom
like the flowers in hand-held bunches,
each word a petal falling
on the fertile soil of ears,
stories pollinate the air,
roots entangle unseen, deep below.

Crutches scrape, a pause:
he watches a young mother,
child clutched like tomorrow's promise,
his smile, a soft fold in time,
acknowledging the cycle:
cradle to crutch, endlessly.

Her basket heavy, not just with goods,
but with the weight of many markets,
each item a chapter,
of sun, rain, frost, and harvest,
her purchase: a choice,
seeded in the soil of need.

Philosophy blooms: quietly,
among the chatter and barter,
the eternal query of existence,
why things grow, fall, rise,
in endless succession,
like day follows a shadowy night.

Stall to stall, life unfurls,
a tapestry woven in real-time,
human spirit threads through,
strong as spider silk,
subtle in the morning's calm,
resilient through the weave of pain.

Begonias spill crimson, violet,
their colors a defiance,
against the drab press of decay,
their blooms a brief rebuttal
   to the tyranny of time,
      loud as a child's cheer.

Coffee steams, breads rise,
   alchemy of heat and hand,
transformations witnessed
in the quiet hum of morning,
  each loaf a soft sculpture,
steam paints the air with aroma.

   This market: a microcosm,
   each soul a star, pulsing
within the constellations of community,
      each interaction a tether,
binding the moment to memory,
the mundane to the magnificent.

Fruits stacked: pyramids,
calling to sun-kissed afternoons,
   juice awaits lips, the burst
     of flavor on the tongue,
     sweet as the first summer day,
ripe with the promise of shade.

Leaves whisper in response,
trees around the market square,
old as some of the stallholders,
witness to countless exchanges,
their roots deep as the lake,
branches high as hopes.

Leaves flutter gently:
a dance of green above stalls,
lake whispers nearby.
The sun casts sharp lines,
shadows stretch into patterns
like thoughts reaching far.

Crowded voices bloom,
overlapping, merging in
a lively chaos.
Hands pick through fresh goods,
colorful yields of the earth:
touch is a language.

He leans on wood crutch,
his eyes reflecting stories
carved deep by the years.
Her basket heavy,
as if carrying seasons
that refuse to end.

Trace of a wrinkle:
lines that time etches slowly,
mapping life's journey.
A smile flickers,
resisting like a candle

in a quiet storm.
Tuberous begonias,
colors bold against the gray,
life persists in blooms.
    Scent of coffee mingles
with the earthiness of bread,

morning's warm embrace.
Stands hold treasures rare,
each object a universe,
crafted by worn hands.
Market conversations:
      humanity in exchange,

priceless yet common.
Old man recounts tales,
voice a soft weave of fabric,
    threadbare but cherished.
    Children's laughter pierces

the hum of gathered voices,
light in dense fog.
Fruits spill from baskets,
abundance in simple form,
    nectar of the sun.
    Her steps speak struggle,

yet grace is in her bearing,
a dance of strong will.
   Connections form here,
in the give and take of life,
each face a mirror.
Cycles of seasons,

reflected in human eyes:
spring yields to winter.
Why does the old fade,
making room for new growth,
cycle evergreen?

Underneath the sky,
I ponder these deep currents,
waves unseen but felt.
Market's vibrant pulse,
beats a rhythm of ages,
ebb and flow of lives.

Nature's own motifs,
repeated in our stories,
woven tightly knit.
Affliction carves paths,
routes of pain and healing both,
strength in creased maps.

Hands exchange goods, smiles:
transactions of deeper ties,
links unseen but felt.
Crutches tap the ground,
steady as a drumbeat, slow,

marking each step's weight.
Her laughter rings out,
a chime against the soft wind,
melody of life.
Vegetables stacked high,
colors dazzling under sun,

palette of the soil.
He touches ripe fruit,
gentle as a lover's kiss,
tenderness in age.
We navigate paths,
between stalls, through seasons,

each step a story.
Bread's aroma fills
the air, yeast and warmth combine,
comfort in each loaf.
Lake reflects the sky,

mirror of infinite loops,
water and cloud dance.
Life's tenacity,
witnessed in each small exchange,
greeting and farewell.
Fragility shows

in the bending of branches,
yet they do not break.
Strength in the quiet,
like roots holding the earth tight,
silent yet mighty.
Ephemeral joys,

captured in glances, fleeting,
yet deeply etched in.
Eternal cycles,
seen in the turnover of
seasons, life, and death.

Market day wanes slow,
shadows lengthen, voices dim,
tapestry complete.
Resilience breathes,
in the stalls, in every step,
market's heart beats strong.

Crumbs tell of meals shared,
stories told around tables,
communion of souls.
Her eyes alight with
memories, crinkling corners,
time's soft signature.

The weight of the years,
carried in baskets, on backs,
endured with each step.
Sunset paints the lake,
golden hues blend into night,
day folds into dreams.

In the hands of June,
the market spills:
colors vibrant as dawn,
fragrances twining,
air rich with chatter,
the lake whispers softly.

Under this sky's broad sweep,
people shuffle, their faces
etched with stories of suns
they have weathered, storms
they have braved, and smiles,
light flickering in their depth.

A woman, changed since fall,
moves with a delicate might,
her body a note in the vast
symphony of existence:
how resilience shapes her,
guiding each determined step.

Nearby, an old man leans
on timeworn crutches,
his pace a testament
to the scars that mark
the battles won silently,
endurance his quiet song.

This place, this moment
binds the fleeting dance
of greetings, laughter spilling,
and memories that echo
in the crackle of voices,
old friends reconnecting.

Why does nature insist
on relentless renewal,
on the ceaseless decay
that ushers forth life anew?
In this cycle, a thread—
unseen, yet palpable—connects.

Every interaction, fleeting,
yet imbued with the weight
of the eternal, captures
the dual nature of existence:
how we are both fleeting
and forever in the same breath.

With the scent of begonias,
mixed with the earthy aroma
of freshly baked bread,
I am reminded of the dance
between strength and fragility,
each step an echo of life's pulse.

Stalls brimming with produce,
hands exchanging goods,
a canvas of human endeavor,
where every color, every texture
tells of labor, love, and loss—
a microcosm of shared fate.

Elderly hands cradle young shoots,
the old giving way to new,
in this cycle, a beauty,
a sorrow, a relentless push
toward what comes next,
nature's inexorable script.

Here, amid the hum of life,
the calls of merchants,
the soft laughter of children,
we see the mirror of the world,
in this small gathering,
the entirety of human experience.

Lines of life run deep,
in the faces, in the hands,
in the exchange of glances,
each bearing the imprint
of years, of joys, of grief—
all within the market's embrace.

Continuing through rows,
each stall a chapter,
each vendor a storyteller,
crafting tales through goods,
through the sweat on their brows,
through the pride in their eyes.

As the lake gently laps
at the edges of this scene,
its rhythm a calming constant,
like the heartbeat of the earth,
I wander, a spectator
in this theatre of the everyday.

The resilience of life,
in its most unassuming forms,
challenges the tempests,
stands defiant against the gales,
each smile, each crease,
a victory, a rebellion.

Continuous and unbroken,
the thread of existence weaves
its way through the market,
connecting each life, each story,
in the web of shared being,
in the dance of intertwined destinies.

Amidst this bustling tableau,
I find the core of humanity,
the relentless spirit that binds
each to all, the collective heartbeat
that pulses strong, even
in the face of fleeting days.

At a stall decked with flowers,
bright petals against green,
I pause: here is life, unabashed,
bold in its bloom, defiant
in its burst of color,
against the gray of worn paths.

A child's laughter breaks
the hum, a clear bell
in the quiet morning,
reminding us that joy,
too, is a form of resistance,
a light that never fully dims.

The continuity of generations,
seen in the handing of an apple,
from wrinkled hand to smooth palm,
encapsulates the cycle of life,
where every ending crafts
the beginning of another story.

As the market throbs
with the life of a community,
its pulse the rhythm of shared
days and communal nights,
I find myself reflecting
on the nature of human connection.

Each stall, each item,
a dot in the constellation
of human endeavor,
mapping out the vast expanse
of our collective journey,
through the cosmos of daily life.

Unscripted Earth

Curled petals: a droplet,
reflecting sky's vast arc,
caught mid-descent: life's web,
interwoven with light—
A leaf's tremble: subtle,
tells of the breezy kiss,

soft upon its green cheek,
invisible yet clear—
Scent of damp earth rises,
a quiet assertion:
life persists underfoot,
murmuring deep secrets—

These are the quiet beats,
the pulse beneath our feet,
the unnoticed rhythms,
language of the living—
The robin's evening hymn,
layers upon our craft,

its melody simple,
piercing the word-clutter—
Yet, we shield ourselves in
barricades of phrases,
each word a brick: walls built
to hide us from the sun—

Our discourse: a river,
turning wild lands docile,
its current strong, shaped by
banks of arranged stone words—
In my own garden's heart,
words become translucent,

each term a prism, split
the light into spectra—
    Spirea blossoms shed
  their white against the soil:
contrast, stark, soft, profound,
ephemeral beauty—

How does the chipmunk think?
In spirals of instinct,
in seamless fits of pulse,
not bound by syntax's yoke—
Seeds tucked within its cheeks,
a simple, vital act,

far removed from the noise
of our endless discourse—
    Yet here I stand, word-bound,
attempting to capture
the essence of wind's touch:
a folly of my kind—

    How do we bridge this gap,
      where words cease to suffice,
    where they falter, stumble,
on nature's simple truth?
Our language: a tool, yes,
but blunted by its breadth,

    overwhelmed by its depth,
in shadows it creates—
Each sentence casts a shade,
    a silhouette of thought,
balancing what's spoken
against the unsaid mass—

Is there a dialect,
a lexicon, unmade,
that sings with the robin,
rustles with the dry leaves?
Could we then speak in hues,
in scents, in shadows cast,

in the soft rush of streams,
in the fox's silent tread?
I explore this idea,
mind roaming as feet tread
over soft, yielding earth,
pondering the unsaid—

Each step a soft imprint,
a language of contours,
more felt than articulated,
a dance with gravity—
The garden is both text
and texture, a manuscript

authored by countless hands,
weathered, alive, speaking—
Underneath, worms navigate
through dark, rich manuscripts,
their passages silent,
devoid of pretense, pure—

Above, the maple spreads,
ambitious in its reach,
leaves filtering sunlight,
a canopy of calm—
What script can capture this,
the silent majesty,

the quiet strength contained
in each reaching limb's curve?
The sky shifts, clouds adrift,
a slow, graceful recast:
light dims, horizon blurs,
day's words dissolve to dusk—

The garden's air thickens,
musk of after-rain: dense,
a fragrance unspoken,
yet fully understood—
How vast the gap between
our crafted narratives

and the stark, wild rhythms
of the earth's own heartbeats—
As night's veil descends soft,
a blanket of quiet,
my thoughts turn inward, seek
the spaces between words—

For there, in the silence,
unshaped by human hands,
   lies the raw truth of earth,
a narrative unspun—
No letters, no pages,
      just the endless hum, pulse,

the unbound, wordless song,
resonating, profound—
      This garden teaches me,
each visit a lesson:
to listen, to observe,
to be still and absorb—

A communion, silent,
beyond our speech's reach,
    where true understanding
blooms, unfettered, rooted—
So I stand, dusk around,
breathing in the cool air,

   letting go of the need
to name each scent, each shade—
Instead, I feel: deeply,
the weight of existence,
the push of burgeoning
life, quiet, insistent—

Continuing to walk,
each step a syllable
in an older language,
spoken by leaf and stone—
Here, in the whispered dark,
words begin to shed weight,

becoming as light as
   the soil's moist, black embrace—
And perhaps, in this space,
our narratives might find
their place, not as rulers,
but as humble pilgrims—

Each word a careful step
on a path well-trodden,
beside the silent speech
  of earth's vast, vibrant tome.
   Beneath the weighty words:
I tread the damp sod:

each step a murmur,
echoes of the treaded path:
these symbols we toss,
airy as spore prints,
they strain to mesh
with the mesh: true forms,

shapes that breathe and pulse,
in the humus-rich dusk,
where the chipmunk darts,
frantic with the bounty
of a hard day's quest:
its small existence

a counterpoint to speech,
and above, the maple—
wide arms open to sky,
taking the sun's offering,
turning brightness
into life's green currency:

each leaf a solar cell,
a factory of air and sustenance.
Our words don't feed
on light, don't drink of rain,
nor thicken with the season's run.
Yet, we speak as if

to conjure spring from soil,
to command the robin's throat
to swell with song,
song that spills unbidden.
For what are words
but signs we strain to see through,

a squall that blurs the lines
between the seen
    and what we say we see?
  Our talk: a network
as tangled as roots beneath,
    often missing the wet slap

of real against our faces,
the slap that wakes,
    that stirs the mud to speak
  in its own tongue,
untranslated, rough,
telling of the dark

where worms weave
through silent dialogues,
    and decay feeds the fresh:
  cycles clipped
by the crispness of our alphabets,
our need to nail down the fluid.

Stalks push through
the crust of hardened lexicon,
  breaking the cool barrier
with raw heads,
humble yet defiant blooms:
the garden a text we read

      wrongly at times,
    our interpretations hung
on the thin trellis
    of our crafted scripts,
so sure of the scaffold,
    yet the vine sprawls

where it will, wild
in the encroach of its arcs,
beyond our penned circles.
Words: a barrage
against the quiet earth,
yet the earth speaks

in a voice that rumbles
deep beneath our feet,
a thrum felt more than heard,
a resonance that stirs
the seeds we have yet
to name, to catalogue,

to reduce to data,
thus they grow, unnamed,
unplotted on our charts,
they grow regardless
of our need to know,
to hold within our lines,

and as twilight deepens,
pulling its soft cloak
around the shoulders
of the hill, the narrative
we've spun unravels,
thread by thread,

into the fabric of night,
where dreams are the dew
that settle on the mind's grass,
whispering other truths,
the truths that rustle
in the leaf's whisper,

in the stalk's nod,
in the bud's tight clench:
unscripted, yet eloquent,
the language of chlorophyll
    and cuticle, of root hair
and nectar, each a word

in the green glossary
    of survival, of flourish,
where meaning blooms
    wildly, not in the confines
of our lines, but in the open,
where breath is more

than something spoken.
In this choreography
of wing, petal, claw,
and leaf, where is the space
    for the thin tracery
  of our thought?

We overlay maps on the landscape,
words on the wild, blind often
  to the subtle contours,
    the hidden valleys
of existence that resist
our script. Yet still,

we write, we layer,
we build our babels
of babel, towers of talk,
believing in the bridge of jargon,
    missing the simple bridge
of a log across a stream,

solid with the silence
of being, the underfoot
solidity that needs no footnote,
no glossary to understand
its place in the scheme,
in the weave of wild,

where each thread is integral,
each silence a part of the symphony,
each note played
by the unseeable hand
of the world, turning,
turning in its ringed dance,

a dance we join unwittingly,
with heavy boots or light,
each step a signature,
an impression in the loam,
each breath a strophe
in the endless poem of earth.

Beneath this shawl of spirea:
their white whispers,
much like words, dissipate:
in the dampness, hovering.
The robin trills, slicing
through evening's canvas:

notes float, unburdened
by syntax's strict chains.
Air, thick with the musk
of nature's soft riot,
speaks in sighs and rustles:
language without letters.

Pathways lined, organic
in their curve, guide
my steps through shadows:
unscripted, freely formed.
Chipmunks, cheeks laden,
dart—nature's errands

never wait for the right phrase:
urgency lost in translation.
Norway maple's arms,
in grand, green arcs,
whisper of world's span
and roots deeper than words.

Even as the mind molds
into neat, aligned thoughts,
the soil scatters its own
rich, unruly verses.
Each petal, a stanza

of fragility echoing strength:
how delicate the balance
that holds both true.
Words cluster—cuneiform,
digital shadows cast long
over the tactile essence

of earth's rough truth.
We layer sentences, sediment
upon the living manuscript:
our footprints, brief edits
in a perennial narrative.
Raindrops, the commas

in the evening's paragraph,
pause the air, saturated
with the grammar of growth.
Dusk falls, punctuated
by the last light: phrases
we fail to capture

in our nets of narration.
Pores of the leaf,
minute gates to vast worlds:
how simple, yet complex,
this photosynthetic dance.

My words attempt to mirror
the precision of nature's mechanisms:
a futile mimic of cycles
that spin seamlessly.
Stems bend, resilient
under the weight of rain—

sentence structures
too rigid would break.
The sparrow's swift dive
is a syntax more eloquent
than our most crafted lines:
effortlessness we can't pen.

Each breath of wind,
an editor's sweeping cut:
clearing the cluttered,
leaving only what must stir.
Twilight, a blending
of color, quiet—soft.

Submerged Dialogues

In the mutter of the stream:
whispers twist: leaves
adrift, caught in the babble
of shallow waters, telling
of depths unsounded: unspoken
truths lie beneath, hidden.

He talks, a leaf upon that stream:
frantic, skimming over
what lies deeper:
scares him, the quiet,
where words end and
meaning begins to swell.

His words, a surface tension,
break with each ripple:
yet below, the calm:
holds secrets tight,
in the grip of still,
dark waters.

I listen, not just to him,
but through him: to
the silence he fences out,
where truth might bloom:
quietly, profoundly,
in spaces left unfilled.

His fear of stillness,
a telltale heart: beating
beneath floorboards:
of spoken things,
each beat echoes:
what's left unsaid.

Words, his maze: labyrinthian,
  paths that twist: turn,
    never center reaching,
where self might lie,
waiting, silent:
   pondering its own shape.

And I, observing,
find my reflection
in his turmoil: see
the stillness shaped
by his constant motion:
a negative space defined.

 Each word he casts—
nets thrown wide:
catching nothing,
yet fearing to come up empty,
   always casting again:
hopeful, desperate.

What fear drives him
to fill every crevice
of air, of time,
   with syllables that flutter
like leaves in wind:
  never landing?

Is it the void he fears,
or what the void might say,
if given voice: if
  silence spoke,
would he, could he,
hear it?

His words wrap around:
the nothing, making it
something to be dealt with,
managed, controlled,
not endured: not
witnessed.

Yet silence has its own speech,
a dialect of pauses:
of breaths taken,
of looks exchanged,
of thoughts unvoiced:
a universe conversing.

In his ceaseless flow,
a river carving landscapes,
he misses the erosion
of his own shores:
how each word spoken
alters him.

I find solace not in words,
but in the lack thereof:
in the quiet left behind
after his torrent subsides,
in the calm that descends:
like dusk on the valley.

The stream flows on,
leaves pass, disappear:
but the water is ever there,
deep, knowing:
a witness to all
that passes, remains.

What might he see
if he dared to look:
beneath the surface,
into the quiet deep,
where words slow,
settle, sediment like truth?

Could he bear the sight
of his unspoken self,
the parts unglossed
by his relentless narrative:
the raw, the real,
the quietly profound?

Perhaps in that silence,
he might find the core
he dances around:
the heart of his being,
not in words,
but in their absence.

Yet he fills every moment,
every breath with
the clutter of sounds,
avoiding the stillness
where true selves
might speak.

So I listen,
to both his words and
the gaps between:
finding in the latter
more substance,
more truth.

His words are leaves on water,
touching everything,
connecting with nothing:
yet beneath, the stream
knows its course,
flows true.

The babble is his shield,
his defense against
the silence he cannot bear,
the unspeakable depth
of his own uncharted waters:
where truth resides.

And yet, this blabbermouth,
in his way, sculpts
monuments to the unsaid,
to all that words
cannot capture:
the essence beyond speech.

In his flight from silence,
he unwittingly praises it:
makes it the thing
most noted, most notable,
in his landscape of verbiage:
the quiet, ever present.

As leaves rush by on the stream,
I find in their fleeting touch
less meaning than in
the water they cover,
deep and still:
holding worlds within.

He speaks to avoid
what lies beneath his words,
but I have come to listen
to what he does not say:
in that silence,
a deeper dialogue unfolds.

In the tumble of words:
traffic, ceaseless and unyielding,
reflects in its haste
the river's hurried pace:
never pausing,
streams flow onward.

Submerged stones, wearing
down to smoother selves,
speak a silent sermon:
endurance shapes
the face of water,
glosses over depths.

Each sentence, his cascade,
muddles the lakebed of thought,
where mud swirls—
and fish dart:
the rapid speech of minnows,
hidden beneath chatter.

A leaf, descending,
meanders; life summarizing
its fall in twists:
captured briefly by the surface,
then swept away—
a momentary tale.

He is the autumn gust:
disturbing placid scenes,
stirring up the fallen,
not to disrupt
the soil's embrace,
but to animate its rest.

His words: twigs snapped
under the hiker's step:
each crack a proclamation,
each pause a place
to plant a seed—
growth in gaps.

Leaves rustle, responding,
not in words, but breaths
of movements; their dance
a counter to his noise,
each sway a subtle tone—
a quieter speech.

Thoughts scatter like seeds
in wind: no pattern,
no plan, yet fertile
with potential paths:
where they land, roots
might take hold.

Stones in the stream
impose no sound,
yet alter flow, creating
eddies, currents: unseen,
yet profoundly felt—
change, the constant.

Beneath his torrent, stones
of silence grow smooth,
reflecting skipped light,
 briefly seen before
  submerging again—
depths hinted, unspoken.

Through layers of murmur,
   forest whispers emerge:
the soft language of leaf
   and loam, where truth
settles like dew—
absorbed, not spilled.

  Each word a leaf
 on the water, momentarily
  alight, then gone—
part of a greater cycle,
  drawn in by currents,
   absorbed by vast seas.

As crickets' twilight calls
 meld into night's onset,
his flurry of phrases
  fades into stars' quiet twinkling—
each a point of light,
   isolated but part of constellations.

His fear of silence underlies
 the flurry: a child's night terror
  banished with babble,
a lantern held
   against the encroaching dark—
light wavering but present.

Observing, I gather
not just his words
but the spaces they skirt,
the contours of silence,
    shaped by sound, defined
by its absence.

The brook understands:
it fills the air with its own
    rushing narrative,
  a story told in perpetuity—
always present,
always past.

Wind converses with foliage,
a low, rustling dialect,
that speaks of change—
    imperceptible yet relentless,
altering landscapes
with a breath.

  Amidst his endless stream,
I am the stone—
creating ripples,
yet deeply rooted,
a part of the stream,
    shaped by its flow.

His monologue, a leaf blower's
roar: clearing paths,
unsettling the settled,
a necessary chaos
that leaves clarity—
   detritus aside, path clear.

Continuously, the circuit
of his thoughts rounds:
never quite touching
the nucleus of quiet—
orbiting a center
laden with unspoken.

Each word, a brushstroke
        in an impressionist painting—
seemingly random,
yet part of a broader hue,
vibrant with intention,
blurring into perception.

Nature whispers back
in every shaded pause,
in every gap he fills—
a dialogue not between voices,
but between sound and hush,
        resonance and retreat.

    And in this flux, I witness
a symphony of absences,
each rest as vital
as the notes that rise,
        each silence a measure
in a greater composition.

He prevents a drought of discourse,
        overflowing, lest we thirst—
but the well is deeper,
fed by quieter springs,
      nurtured in the dark—
rich with the unvoiced.

His fear: a surface tension,
keeping the deep at bay,
words like leaves on water,
skimming over what lies beneath—
never diving,
  never still.

Yet, in his flood, nutrients:
   soil stirred, seeds dispersed,
    growth incited by the chaos
  of his passing storm—
a landscape watered,
    reluctantly fertile.

Each notion, a pebble tossed
into the pond of public thought,
ripples emanating—
reaching far shores,
    disturbing sediment,
unsettling the settled.

His cascade: a metaphor
for nature's own processes—
eroding here, depositing there,
    an endless reshaping
     of landscapes, both mental
and earthen.

  And thus, I observe,
not just to hear, but to see—
beyond the barrage,
through the veil of velocity,
to where still waters run,
    deep and dark.

Tuning into the undertones,
  the subtext of the breeze,
the narrative beneath the noise,
where meaning molds itself
in the silence—
spoken in the unspoken.

    His barrage: a river in flood,
banks breached,
spilling over, inundating,
yet nourishing in its overflow—
chaotic, yet crucial,
    life-giving in its inundation.

From this, I draw my reflections:
mirrored in the flow,
    seen in the fleeting,
understood not through capture,
but through contemplation—
the art of listening, submerged.

His words: not barriers,
  but bridges, ephemeral yet essential,
spanning the gaps
within us, between us—
connecting more in their crossing
than in their content.

And as the day closes,
the stream calms,
the babble blends into night's quiet,
    a completeness found
in the cycle's close—
silence speaks last.

Cycle of Continuance

crumbled leaves stir:
here, the wind brings:
messages encoded:
in the dance of:
decay, whispering a
tale of renewal:

molecules disperse,
become air, soil,
water: a cycle of
endless becoming,
twisting: life clings
desperately to life:

as shadows deepen,
the half-light magnifies
every silent drama:
a leaf breaking down,
its edges curling,
life now dust:

in this twilight,
anticipation breeds
in the chill: the earth
prepares for the silent
alchemy of night,
transforming cold:

beneath my feet,
microcosms thrive:
curling roots gripping,
soil enriched by
yesterday's debris:
life thrives upon death:

my breath clouds
in cool air: each exhale
feeds hungry plants,
while I inhale their
gift of oxygen:
exchange is life:

above, stars blink:
distant furnaces burning:
their light tells stories
of ancient births,
explosions, and fade-outs:
we are made of star-stuff:

and in this vast expanse,
amid the rustle of leaves,
the persistence of ants,
the stalking cat, the
scavenging dog, there
is symphony in survival:

each creature, each cell,
plays its part in this
grand orchestration:
nothing is wasted,
every drop of dew
has a purpose:

the quiet night holds
all our complexities,
our fears, doubts,
joys, nestled in the
dark like seeds
awaiting spring's kiss:

twilight deepens,
and in this hush,
moments saturate:
rich with the musk
of damp earth, the
sharp tang of pine:

what secrets do these
simple scenes hold?
depths unplumbed by
our daily heedlessness,
wonders right beneath
our too-busy feet:

and so, amid these cycles,
where each ending
breeds beginnings, I
stand, contemplating
the continuous thread:
existence weaves:

as night claims territory,
from the fading edges
of day, I am struck
by the quiet majesty
of simple existence,
complex in its simplicity:

soil under fingernails,
I sense the bond, the
heritage we share with
all that grows, decays,
transforms: the humble
majesty of dirt:

and looking up,
the stars gaze down,
impassive, distant, yet
somehow part of this
same narrative: cosmic
spectators to our play:

the wind picks up,
a sigh across the land,
carrying the scent of
rain on its breath,
promising a nurturing
for tomorrow's growth:

what lessons lie
in the mundane:
the meal scraps,
the empty containers,
ours but a moment,
then earth's forever:

in this cycle,
each object, each moment
is a dollop of eternity,
shared among billions,
carried on the backs
of beetles and ants:

nothing is too small,
too insignificant in
the grand scheme:
each part necessary,
beautiful in its duty,
sacred in its role:

the night deepens,
and with it, my thoughts:
how intertwined are our
fates with these tiny
dramas unfolding in
the underbrush:

each rustle, each
    movement a testament
to the persistence of
  life: in every corner,
under every leaf, there
is a story of survival:

    as the earth turns,
and the night wears on,
I stand amid these
cycles of consumption,
renewal, the endless
    dance of creation and decay:

   these thoughts, these
observations, are but
echos of nature's
wisdom: telling us
  that nothing ends,
    everything transforms:

  and as the first hints
of dawn color the
 eastern sky, I realize
    how much remains
undiscovered, how
richly layered our world:

the cycle continues,
unending, each moment
    a link in an eternal chain:
a breathing, thriving
whole, where even the
smallest role matters:

as light returns,
gilding leaves and
waking sleepers, I
feel renewed, part of
something larger,
  immersed in life's flow:

  with each sunrise,
new chances: for growth,
for learning, for seeing
  the familiar anew,
for embracing the role
we play in this vast tapestry:

the day begins:
a fresh page in
the earth's journal,
   written by a thousand
hands, seen through
a thousand eyes:

what will today hold,
as I walk these paths,
touch these leaves,
feel the pulse of
  the living earth
beneath my feet:

how wondrous,
to be a note in this
grand symphony,
to sing with the rustling
trees, the whispering wind,
the chirping birds:

each moment a stitch
in the fabric of time,
binding us to each
other, to the cycles
of the stars, the moon,
the ever-turning earth:

as I walk on,
the path unwinds before me,
rich with the echoes
of yesterday, whispering
promises of tomorrow,
sweeping me along:

and I realize,
as I blend into the
landscape, that I, too,
am a leaf on this mighty
tree of life, transient
yet eternal in nature's heart:

here, in the dance
of light and shadow,
of growth and decay,
we find the true rhythm
of existence, the deep
melody of the cosmos:

every end a beginning,
every silence a prelude
to new music: thus
we continue, part of
the unending song,
echoing through the ages:

so let us listen,
let us observe,
let us be attuned
to the subtle shifts,
the small whispers
of the earth's teachings:

for in each minute detail,
in each ordinary moment,
there is extraordinary
beauty, there is the
whole universe speaking,
if only we learn to hear:

let this day be
a testament to the
unseen, to the often
ignored splendor of the
mundane, the everyday:
let us find awe in the familiar:

and as the sun climbs,
so does my heart,
each beat a drumming
of syncopated rhythms
with the world around me,
alive, vibrant, resonant:

and so it goes,
the endless cycle,
the beautiful, intricate
dance of life and death,
of decay and renewal,
forever woven into time:

thus, in the leavings
of day's end, in the
consumed and discarded,
there is always a beginning,
a seed of tomorrow,
  nestled in today's heart:

  and standing here,
I feel a part of it all,
  a witness to the cycles,
  connected by breath,
by life, by the constant
  turning of worlds:

the day wanes,
shadows stretch,
and in this cycle, I find
  a profound simplicity,
a soothing rhythm in
the pulse of the universe:

as dusk approaches,
I'm reminded that each
  day's end is but a prelude
  to the night's quiet symphony,
a pause before the renewal
offered by starlit dreams:

and through it all,
the relentless flow of time,
the dance of light, the
echoes of creation, I am
part of this narrative,
woven into the cosmos's fabric:

an observer, a participant,
a scribe of fleeting moments,
standing amid the ceaseless
turning of days into nights,
finding solace in the
continuum of existence:

for here, in the cycle,
in the turning of the soil,
in the rhythm of the seasons,
lies the truth of our being,
the essence of our connection
to the perennial, eternal flow:

and as night falls again,
the stars re-emerge,
each a point of light in
the vast, indifferent cosmos,
guiding our thoughts back
to the infinite, to the eternal:

thus ends the day,
and with it, one cycle of
our ceaseless inquiry,
one arc in the endless
orbit of our existence,
spiraling into tomorrow:

and always, the earth beckons,
asking us to notice, to engage,
to be part of the grand tale
it tells, whispering through
the tree boughs, the rustling
leaves, the silent stars:

for in each ending, there is a
beginning, in each decay, a
renewal; thus, the world teaches
us, in its infinite permutations,
the enduring beauty of transformation:
    embracing this, I step forward,

into the night, carrying the lessons
of the day, the wisdom of the earth,
    the stars above guiding my way,
ever onward, into the cycle of ages:
  each step a testament, each breath
a proclamation: life persists,

in myriad forms, through countless
    iterations, always moving, always
becoming: this is the nature of things:
and as I pause, under the vast sky,
I realize that this, too, is a part of
    Each day we peel away:

layers of fruit skin,
tin lids, broken seals,
as ants march in a line,
algorithmic, attuned,
to the scent of decay.
In the turning earth,

microbes feast silently,
transforming waste,
their secret banquet
beneath the skin of soil—
this, too, is a rebirth.
Paper thins in rain,

ink bleeds away:
words lost, or maybe
freed from the confines
of their printed borders,
mingling with mud.
Molecules in flux,

nature's ledger keeps
a precise account:
nothing lost, everything
transformed, borrowed
momentarily by us.
A leaf's journey from

branch to ground tells
a tale of seasons:
each fall, a surrender,
each spring, a return,
endlessly cycled.
We are part of this,

walking between
birth and decay,
our own bodies
a temporary alignment
of countless elements:
the spent light bulbs.

Rumors of Change

In the calm drizzle, I stood:
pondering life's frail outlines,
  its unexpected ruptures:
a leaf, once verdant, now
crisp in autumn's turn,
  speaking of cycles, of ends.

An ant struggles with a twig:
its burden larger than
its tiny, determined form,
    mirroring our own loads,
heavy with gathered grief,
a journey through rough paths.

Clouds loom, a gray assembly:
quiet observers of turmoil,
  carrying storms yet withholding,
like minds brimming with thoughts
yet silent in the tempest
of societal storms brewing.

The wind whispers secrets,
carried from distant mountains,
telling tales of ancient stones,
  weathered but still standing:
resilience etched in their cores,
much like the human spirit.

Water gathers in soil's embrace,
seeping, life-giving, or
suddenly torrential in floods,
each droplet a narrative
of nourish or destroy,
duality in existence's flow.

Roots reach deep and wide,
  hidden, yet vital for the stand,
like unseen bonds of love,
supporting when seen foundations
quake, and visible strengths falter,
preserving life against odds.

A hawk slices the sky's vastness,
its flight a graceful hunt,
   eyes sharp on the unseen,
  focused: a single point of survival,
against the vast, indifferent blue,
nature's own fierce focus.

  Leaves rustle with rumors of change,
summer's bright green dims
into the gold of coming chill,
 a spectral, slow transformation,
 not unlike our gradual aging,
barely noticed, yet profound.

The river, a relentless carver,
shapes its destined path with
both gentle flows and fierce floods,
   carrying the wisdom of the mountains,
   to the depths of an endless ocean,
   life's lessons in constancy and adapt.

 Sunset casts golden threads,
weaving day into dusk,
  a tapestry hung briefly
before night's dark curtain falls,
 each ending a prelude to
  a new stage, yet unseen.

Stars punctuate the heavens,
sharp points in the soft black,
each a fiery testament
to enduring light amidst darkness,
guiding wandering thoughts
like beacons in vast uncertainty.

Moths dance in lamplight's lure,
drawn to a deceptive safety,
their tiny wings beating patterns
of hope against the perils,
a fluttering persistence in
the face of lurking shadows.

Frogs croon a night's melody,
songs swelling in damp air,
an ancient chorus of wetlands,
echoing through reeds and rushes,
a resilient symphony,
persistent through encroaching silence.

Dew collects in silent hours,
jewels laid upon morning's ground,
each droplet reflecting first light,
transforming into bright clarity,
a renewal, each day's subtle promise,
rebirth in the quiet dawn.

Thus wander I, through nature's script:
reading lines of life and decay,
each a verse in the eternal poem,
where personal pains meet
the universal, where each step
may tread on shadows or light.

And so the journey goes,
paths diverge and wind,
leading to horizons unseen,
with each footfall, a story,
woven into the vast, intricate
tapestry of existence, ongoing.

In this vast weave, I find
not just paths, but intersections,
where others' footprints cross mine,
sharing direction, if only briefly,
each encounter a stitch binding
moments into shared memory.

The wind rises once more,
carrying away the fallen leaf,
the severed twig, the worn stone,
reminders that nothing holds
forever, yet in release,
there lies a form of solace.

Night folds its cloak gently,
over the landscape of thought,
in its dark folds, I find
not fear, but a deep resonance
with the earth's unlit mysteries,
where hidden growth germinates.

Thus, in nature's endless book,
I read, I learn, I reflect,
finding in each fallen leaf,
in every quiet stone, a part
of the vast, intertwining narrative,
tying me to the world, to life.

The journeys of days,
threaded with the journeys within,
lead to the same conclusion:
    that all paths, lit or darkened,
converge in the heart's quiet
corners where truths are whispered.

  Each whisper a ripple on the surface,
  disturbing the stillness briefly,
sending forth waves that may
touch other lives, in unseen ways,
  a gentle impact, spreading wide
from a single, small stone's drop.

In this broad expanse,
where thoughts meld with the horizon,
    where the sky meets the land
in an embrace of possibilities,
I find the courage to stand,
witness to the cycles, participant.

    Time ticks in leaf's descent,
in the ant's relentless march,
in the river's patient sculpting,
a reminder that in every moment,
the world remakes itself,
   and we, unwitting, do the same.

    As dawn breaks anew,
on fields wet with dew's kiss,
   on forests hushed in mist's embrace,
I walk on, a silent observer,
a ponderer of puzzles,
  a seeker of the seamless thread.

Endings are but illusions,
mere pauses in the long narratives
that nature recites in her sleep,
and awakens to repeat,
each day a reincarnation,
each night a quiet reflection.

In this cycle, I find a comfort,
a steady pulse beneath chaos,
a rhythm to which my own
beats can harmonize, quietly,
steadily, amid the ever-turning
wheel of stars, of seasons, of self.

Here, the journey does not cease,
but deepens, each step a deeper
imprint on the soft earth of time,
each breath a mingling
of my air with the world's,
a shared respiration, life's quiet dialogue.

And in this dialogue,
I find not answers, plain and neat,
but rather questions, leading to
more winding paths, under stars,
beside rivers, through forests,
where the questions are the journey.

The oak stands firm,
witness to centuries,
its bark a tableau of resilience,
its roots a network, complex,
a silent testament to strength,
gathered slowly, grain by grain.

And under such a canopy,
I pause, reflect on the fleeting
nature of human endeavors,
how our own roots are tangled,
our own stories woven
into the larger, living loom.

Leaves whisper, a soft susurrus,
carrying tales of gentle decay,
of vibrant life, of seasons' shift,
a language of the perpetual,
spoken in the green tongues
of leaf, of blade, of blooming petal.

Such is the text of the world,
a script in perpetual edit,
where each life adds a line,
a comma, a period, a breath,
in the ongoing story,
ever unfolding, ever evolving.

And in this evolution,
I find my peace, my place,
a note in the grand symphony,
resonating with the chords
of falling leaves, rushing waters,
the deep music of the earth.

Thus, I walk on,
a part of all I have passed,
and all that passes through me,
in this grand, intricate dance
of existence, where each step
is both an arrival and a departure.

In the quiet solitude of nature,
where the pulse of life beats palpable,
I am both lost and found,
a wanderer who at once
sees the path and forges it anew,
with each breath, each thought, each step.

This is the journey, unending,
a loop of seasons, of thoughts,
of ceaseless beginnings and soft ends,
where every conclusion is merely
a pause, a breath taken,
before the next step, the next word.

And in the seamless joining,
of leaf to twig, of night to day,
of self to the swirling cosmos,
I find not the end, but the path,
winding, true, and ever before me,
beckoning with quiet insistence.

This is the dance, the rhythm,
nature's own heartbeat,
to which I add my own,
a syncopation in the vast melody
of existence, where each note
matters, each silence speaks.

With each step, I tread
on the bones of the old,
on the sprouts of the new,
in the ever-turning cycle,
where endings are beginnings,
and beginnings lead to ends.

Such is the cycle I walk,
a path laid by countless feet,
each bearing their own tales,
each step a mark, a memory,
in the soft earth of existence,
each one a declaration: I am here.

As night deepens, stars brighten,
casting light on my thoughts,
each a reflection of the other,
the celestial and the cerebral,
where the universe expands
and so too does

Lost potential, like seeds that
sprout only to be crushed: how
I seek solace in the scattered,
the broken, subdued by the wheel
of the relentless mundane,
where truth is buried deep.

Each vein in a leaf, a tale
of growth, of life pulsing,
reaching out through space,
spider-web thin and just as fragile,
holding droplets of reality
that shatter, reflecting vastness.

The universe bends, unfurls
like ferns in moist shade,
coding secrets in the curl
of their ancient spirals,
whispers of what might be
if only we could hear.

Time itself seems to slow,
each second a dripping tap,
falling through the quiet
of a world too loud to let
the soft thud of water
echo the beats of our hearts.

Caught in the creases of
skin, are stories crumpled,
wrinkled narratives, telling
of the folds of pain, love,
the worn paths tears made,
and the smiles that creased sunsets.

Particles—atoms split and
dance in the endless ballet
of existence, never touching,
yet bound by invisible forces,
a metaphor for the distances
that keep us apart yet bind us.

Such is the paradox we live:
finding connection in isolation,
discovering joy in fragments
of shared despair, where light
dances on the edges of shadows,
shaping darkness into beauty.

And now, in softer tones,
the earth speaks of renewal,
of cycles that spin, weave,
patterns in the loom of time,
where endings are but pauses
before the next breath begins.

Is it not strange how pain
illuminates the paths of joy,
   how the sting of loss carves
  out the caverns for new rivers
to flow, serene, carrying
the debris of past lives?

In this dance of contrast,
where dark yields to light,
the sweet ache of existence
finds its rhythm, beats out
a melody of was and will be,
the song of ongoingness.

Amidst all, the slow decay
of a father, the erosion
  of memories, sharp once,
now blunted by the passage
of relentless days, silent
in their persistent march.

Here, I find myself pondering,
the fragile intersections
of life's sprawling maze,
where each turn might reveal
a new shade of the known,
     a different hue of the truth.

Pause here, by the water,
watch the reflection ripple—
each wave a soft goodbye,
a gentle reminder of flow,
of all that passes, yet
leaves its mark on the shores.

Look how the light breaks,
upon the surface, fracturing
into a thousand radiant paths,
each a possible journey,
a fragmented exploration
into the heart of light itself.

And so, we wander, lost
yet found in every step,
each imprint a testament
to the paths taken,
the choices made, the quiet
rebellion against the inevitable.

Across the mind's sky, thoughts drift:
like wind-swept clouds
not tethered, free to roam,
intersecting with the clarity
of day's bright trials;
each cloud a muse's whisper.

The trees stand witness:
bark grooved with age,
roots tangled beneath,
sucking life—sustained
by Earth's sweet draught;
the whole earth a body alive.

Leaves chatter in twilight's breeze:
words unformed, but ripe
with latent messages—
each flutter a soft heartbeat,
each rustle a breath drawn:
nature converses in sighs.

Interwoven Cycles

Leaves shift overhead:
branches, too, move subtly,
demanding notice:
but why this dance, this silent,
sway: is it merely for
air's sake, or something deeper,

a slow respiration?
Tiny flecks of light seep through,
revealing spots of
soft, dappled ground: patches where,
perhaps, seeds may decide
to plunge roots: an optimism,

basic, yet profound.
Each leaf, a tiny solar cell,
working, converting:
photosynthesis—a marvel,
complex, yet so clean.
In this light, this very moment,

a clarity comes:
cycles of living, dying,
the energy flows,
uninterrupted, seamless,
a pattern so grand.
And underfoot, the soil keeps

secrets, harbors seeds:
a microcosm of the vast
networks in the forest,
interconnected, reliant
on each silent act.
Here, a bird's leftover matter,

insignificant,
becomes nourishment: nothing,
in nature, wasted,
each atom recycled,
part of a greater whole.
   The bird, aloft, sees landscapes,

   not as we see them:
but as fields of possibility,
patterns, textures,
a mosaic of ecosystems,
living, breathing.
And so, my smeared fingers now

seem less an insult,
more a reminder: we touch,
change things, always,
even without knowing:
impact is inevitable.
Each step along this path marks

a new interaction,
a transfer of energy:
     soft soil compressed,
a leaf turned, a stone nudged,
quiet disturbances.
Yet, are these changes lasting?

Does the path remember
      my footprints, or does it wait
for rain, to erase,
to return to a state of
unmarked potential?
Continuing onward, I find

rhythm in my steps,
a pace that matches the heartbeat
    of this living land:
each inhale of crisp, cool air,
an exchange, a gift.
A hill rises: its slope a

challenge, yet inviting.
  Every climb a metaphor,
   a journey upwards,
    striving perhaps to see what
the geese view in flight.
At the summit, a pause: breath

heavy, eyes wide, survey:
   the valley stretches, cradles
    the horizon line,
an embrace of earth and sky:
this vast, open poem.
Here, where the sky meets the land,

beauty undeniable,
yet marred, if one chooses to
    see it so, by tracks,
by signs of prior passages,
by life lived and spent.
Strolling down, returning to

where the journey started,
questions linger, like the last
    light on the hillside:
the marks we leave, are they scars,
or are they something more?
Sky's open page, blue and vast,

I walk its lines: no words, just paths.
Bird wings whisper, slight and fast,
Their shadows pass, ephemeral drafts.
A touch of white upon my coat,
Nature's script, a fleeting note.
From lofty heights, what tales float

Down to us, who seldom gloat?
My fingers spread the unexpected
Gift: a residue, now connected
To thoughts of journeys, undetected,
Invisible threads, finely webbed and
Interwoven, like the flights

Of geese, stark against the lights
Of dawn: they thread the air, no sights
Of borders, just the endless flights.
They leave no trace we see, yet change
Is in their wake, range upon range.
Each beat a push, strange rearrangements,

Invisible, yet vast, these exchanges.
The hill's eternal line, a face
Known well to time's unyielding grace,
Speaks of cycles, returns, the base
Rhythms of earth, and our brief place.
Our marks, do they dissolve, wash away

In rains, or will some fragments stay?
Does our touch alter paths, or lay
A new course? Do we lead or stray?
Stains on stone, wind in the leaves,
Each step a story, threads we weave;
The fabric of the earth receives

Our footprints, as the spider perceives
Each tremor in her web, alive
To vibrations: so we strive
To sense our impact, how we drive
Or blend in, whether we'll survive.
The blue expanse, morning's realm,

My thoughts, like clouds, overwhelm.
The subtle art of nature's helm
Guides each leaf, each elm.
Permanence: a myth we chase,
In landscapes, life, each wrinkling face.

Change enfolds us, a tight embrace,
Leaving hints, a subtle trace.
The beauty in marked paths, in stains,
Is in their telling: what remains
Not pristine, but touched, the gains

Of seeing where life's print maintains.
Time's narrative, woven in air,
In soil, in water everywhere,
Tells that all things, foul or fair,
Are linked, a mesh, a communal flare.

As birds navigate skies unseen,
So we traverse life's verdant green,
Each a wanderer, between
The stars and earth, in the vast in-between.
This journey, marked by start and ends,

Is like the bird that descends
Upon my path, its message sends
Rippling through my day, transcends
Simple annoyance or surprise,
Opening up my heart and eyes

To the unscripted, unforeseen ties,
To the myriad ways our world replies.
Every flea that nibbles on a leaf,
Every wave that shapes a reef,
In their actions, brief or chief,

Inscribe the world, its joy, its grief.
Each interaction, push, or merge,
Each border crossed, horizon verge,
Reveals how extensively we surge,
How mixed our paths, our motives, urges.

So I continue, step by step,
Under the sky's expansive web,
Contemplating how we prep
For journeys made, the vast trek.
In essence, everything that's touched

By life, leaves traces, much
As words suggest when they clutch
At meanings, in their tender hush.
And in this walk under the skies
I find the vast books of the wise,

Not in libraries, but in the guise
Of wind and wing, earth's old, deep cries.
Every leaf a page, every tree
A chapter in the saga we
Are writing, just by being free,

By living out our destiny.
Balanced between ephemeral and
Eternal, we stand, expand,
Exploring limits, land by land,
Nature's text in heart, in hand.

across my fingers, stirring
visions unasked for: what
mean these casual marks,
    this silent testimony of
overflights: gulfs and currents,

all wrapped in a feather's
bare touch: the geese know,
    paths etched in the vast
press of sky: each wing-beat
a stroke against the immense

    canvas of the air, where
clouds pattern the narrative
  of journey and pause: ephemeral,
  yet enduring just as every
   breath we take and remake:

what currents uplift them,
invisible yet felt, a dance of
pressure and release: this
   is nature's mechanism: unseen,
yet crucially felt, a force

    that binds the wing to the wind,
the earth to the cloud: thus,
  we walk unaware beneath
the vast canopy of interactions,
a part of the dance we barely

    perceive: how can we fathom
   our place in this flow: are we
mere passersby or crucial to
   the rhythm? our every step,
   a ripple across the surface

of the earth, sending soft
echoes through the crust: each
impact a whisper into the deep's
ear: the soil, rich and dark,
  records our passing, fleeting

yet fixed in its memory: such
is nature: a matrix of action and
    reaction, an endless loop:
so, I ponder these connections,
deep as roots and wide as skies,

  as the residue of flight fades
from my fingers, but not from
    thought: these small instances,
dominoes that fall and flicker
an influence farther than sight,

  further than we imagine: and
the bird, no longer here, yet
its path crosses mine, a brief
intersection of lives: this
  shared space of air and moment,

where our stories overlap,
then diverge: I wonder, then,
of the traces we unknowingly
  leave, seeds sown in the wind,
destinies shaped by silent

droppings: and so, life suggests,
through these accidental meetings,
a network of invisible forces,
connecting and configuring
the puzzle pieces of existence,

into a mosaic grander than
seen by the eye: every element
a pixel in this vast image,
every life a color in the full
spectrum of existence,

where every departure
is an arrival elsewhere,
the world not less for the loss,
but different: continuous,
a shifting shape of realities,

as geese fly in formation,
each taking a turn at the lead,
relieving the one ahead,
sharing the burden, drafting
in the pull of communal effort,

a metaphor for our own
existences: how we bear,
and are borne, by each other,
in turns we may not foresee,
through storms unseen,

across distances we may
never measure: this fabric of
being, so tightly woven, each
thread reliant on another,
in a strength found in togetherness,

as the landscape unfolds
below the travelers, constant
in its change, a flux that molds,
erodes, builds, and blooms,
a reminder of transience,

yet permanence: the hill's
eternal line, a quiet testament
to endurance, to the realm
of cycles: birth, and rebirth,
    an ongoing dialogue between

the earth and the sky, a
conversation of elements,
echoing the unseen ties,
binding atom to atom, species
  to species, individual to cosmos,

as step echoes step, and thought
reflects thought, in this vast
   theater of existence, where
every actor plays a part,
scripted not by us, but for us,

and we, improvising within
the outlines drawn by nature,
find our lines, speak our
pieces, contribute our voices
to the chorus that shapes

the story of life, a tale told
in the language of interconnection,
of dependency and offering,
where each offering feeds
     into the loop of give and take,

    where what is left behind
is not waste, but a resource,
  every end a beginning,
   every closure an opening,
a mosaic of ceaseless creation,

each creature, each element,
a worker in this continuum,
shaping a legacy in subtle
touches: feather on shoulder,
footprint on earth, echo in air,

a continuity wrapped in
the simple and the complex,
a symphony played on the
instruments of existence,
each note essential, resonant,

thus, beneath the open blue,
I walk, a part of the vast,
yet vital pageant, where
every smear, every trace,
tells of connection, of shared fates,

and as I wipe my hand clean,
the sky offers no end,
only vastness, inviting wonder,
pondering, and the endless
journey of thought and being.

Legacy of Layers

in the tangle of
    wires: once pulses raced
    here, messages zipped
     from brain to byte:
a network now
silent, cobwebbed

this plastic shell,
a canopy of dreams
manufactured: now
discarded, it seems
every end a start
  in reverse, unwound

   layers peel from
the composite bones,
an archaeology
    of consumption:
we dig, only to
find, our hollow castoffs

maps of circuits
once alive with light:
   now, pathways for
     the ant, the moss,
a new realm's footprints
over old quests

   each screen, each device
    a fossil record
of desire, fingers
that swiped, tapped:
     a ballet of urgency
now stilled, quieted

these tools, these toys,
extensions of mind
and will, electronic
limbs we outgrew:
or did they outgrow
us, their creators?

we built to save
time, to hold close
every fleeting pulse
of thought, feeling:
yet here, saved time
rots, no longer precious

a motherboard's etched
with silvered paths:
like rivers seen from
the skies, flowing
to some sea we
never reached

batteries leak their
last, acid truths
into the soil, a
harsh afterlife
for what powered
our days

lenses that captured
the light of our lives
now stare blankly at
ceilings, not skies:
their mission obsolete,
a shutter closed

wires that connected
      now tangle, trip
feet walking away
from what was needed,
once, now not:
  our detritus spreads

plastic, metal, glass,
meld in the heap:
a modern midden
telling tales, not
of meals, but of
minds fed too fast

here, a printer carcass,
     there, a cracked phone—
      each a chapter in
the book of progress
      now shelved in the
dust of disregard

a fan hums no more,
blades that cooled
sweat of brows under
      lamps, late, working:
the heat now gone,
the urgency cooled

what remains is
  not merely refuse
but a testament
to reach, to grasp
      beyond our grip:
a reach, now frozen

we crafted these
from ores drawn
from deep veins,
from oil, ancient sunlight
trapped, then transformed:
we burn the buried sunlight

each item a node
in a network of
desire, of aspiration
meshed with fear
of missing out:
our modern moraine

a battery drains its
last volt, final
heartbeat, echo
in a chamber
of commerce:
cold now, energy spent

yet this silence, this
pause, allows whispers
from the earth
itself, soft murmurs
under the clamor
of manufacture

it speaks of cycles,
of leaves that fall
to feed the forest floor,
of water cycled
from sea to cloud
to rain: renewing

but what of plastic?
what of alloys,
elements coaxed
    into unnatural unions,
lovers not meant
to meet, yet merged?

we ponder this,
legacy of layers:
while the wind shifts
  papers, stirs the
ghosts of gadgets,
a soft disassembly

here, amid sprawled
silicon and wire,
a reclamation occurs—
nature, slow, insistent,
begins its patient
alchemy of decay

moss does not discriminate,
greening motherboard
    and metal alike,
    a velvet revolution
soft as a whisper,
loud as a creed

roots probe, pry
into crevices, cracks,
    where hands assembled
but never lingered:
life claims, reclaims
its ancient prerogative

this slow digestion,
a consumption that
 creates as it consumes,
transforms gadget
to humus, artifact
to earth

yet, as we stand
in this quiet aftermath
of our own making,
we face our own
 obsolescences, our
inevitable rust

can we learn,
from leaf, from loam,
 a better blueprint
for our making
and unmaking:
 a sustainability?

in this graveyard
of our gadgetry,
 do we find a
mirror, darkly
reflecting not just
what we've made but us?

 as we sift through
this silicon detritus,
let us seek not
just disposal, but
 discovery: finding
in decay, a new growth

here amid the whispers
of expired circuits,
may we compose
not elegies for
what is lost, but
hymns to what might bloom

this, then, our task:
not only to create
but to understand
the life, and death,
of our creations:
their echoes, their dust

may each thing we make
hold not just the
spark of now, but
the seeds of
new forests, new
fields, nourished by time

thus, we walk amid
the ruins of our
rapid fire desires,
seeking not salvage,
but wisdom in
the wreckage

every end, if seen
with clear eyes,
offers a trail,
a path back
to beginnings:
cycle unbroken

so let us start
again, but with
care, with reverence
for both the ephemeral
and the eternal:
 our footprints, lighter

as the poet, I
probe, ponder, and
parse: each line
 a furrow, sowing
seeds in the soil
of the mind.

Here, in the quiet
aftermath of consumption,
I strive to compose
not just an ode
to what is lost,
but a dialogue with what remains.

 I pick through relics:
whispers of solder,
hard plastic shells,
scraps of silken copper.
Brush the dust
from a CRT face,

 a room in a tube,
dead tech's embrace.
Each piece a maze:
complex circuits' grace,
 past thoughts captured
in now-obsolete space.

These idle gears,
fruits of fervid minds,
once moved with purpose
now silently confined.
Here lies the cassette:
tape tangled, tight,

a music box phantom
that lost its fight.
A tower of CDs,
rainbows under dust,
each one a prism
of dreams and rust.

Towers leaning,
bent softly with age,
stacks of VHS,
paused on life's stage.
An old typewriter,
keys sticky—resist,

echoes of letters,
fates sealed with a twist.
The obsolescence,
a march, relentless,
each artifact a lesson:
impermanence, endless.

A fallen empire of silicon,
capacitors, resistors—
all lie defeated beneath
the shadow of transistors.
A phone with no signal,
a screen cracked, yet brave,

its icons bright fossils
in a silicon grave.
The forgotten cables,
each with a role,
now tangled narratives,
a knotted whole.

A notebook's spine,
cracked, threads bare,
pages of ideas
adrift in stale air.
Each object tells
of its own demise,

a story of neglect,
hidden from eyes.
Beneath the rubble,
potential sleeps,
inertia's blanket,
heavy and deep.

This museum of progress,
a junkyard of dreams,
each gadget a gravestone
for what might have been.
Particles of the past,
a disassembled song,

now mere echoes
of right and wrong.
I pause and consider:
our tangible ghosts,
the weight of our wants,
a consuming host.

How we cast aside
what once was revered,
in pursuit of the new,
the unblemished, the clear.
Reverberations of use,
soundless in halls,

an inventory of extinction,
as each era falls.
Objects once vital,
now mere debris,
a cycle unending,
tech's faded marquee.

Beauty inherent
in the abandoned, the old,
stories untold,
in the silence, they're told.
Can we recover,
resurrect these lost arts,

find new roles for old tools,
repurpose these parts?
Amidst the decay,
new thoughts take flight,
from detritus, creation,
from darkness, light.

From forgotten fragments,
potential springs,
hope in renewal,
what reimagining brings.
Objects, ideas,
all can be mended,

transcending the cycle
where utility ended.
In each discarded device,
a kernel of truth,
lessons on limits,
the follies of youth.

We weave through waste,
a labyrinth dense,
finding paths forward,
a new recompense.
Reclaiming the cast-offs,
the technological spurned,

in their shadows, we glean
what must be learned.
This graveyard of gadgets,
a testament seen,
to the cost of our culture,
our machine dreams.

Yet within this refuse,
a transformation calls,
from old to new,
as renewal enthralls.
The poet, the tinkerer,
together aligned,

in scrapyards discover
the treasures defined.
From ruin to revival,
from waste to rebirth,
reshaping the remnants
found on the earth.

Interwoven Tapestry

Amidst the threads: raw,
woven deep, patterns formed
not by design, but
by the tremulous hands of
nature: the true artist
owning chaos, beauty.

Sunlight fractures along
the crest of morning hills,
a dance of photons,
invisible yet felt warmth,
spreading its gentle touch,
dispersing shadows.

What is this fear but a
tapestry too tightly
wound? Fibers tensing,
contracting against the
loom's fixed and rigid frame,
threatening to snap.

These hills: they erode,
yet they stand, firm despite
the wind's persistent
whispers, rain's erosion,
and seeds that wedge deeply,
breaking stone to soil.

Within the soft murk,
microcosms burst alive,
cellular dances,
mitosis dividing,
root tips seeking moisture:
life's quest continues.

Atoms to molecules,
stars to galaxies: wide
expanses connect
    the vast to the minute,
declaring independence
    from simplicity.

Phobias: mind's mire,
where dread and wonder conflate,
    dark with luminous,
a dichotomy that feeds
growth, molds fear into the
    quest for understanding.

Every leaf, each drop
of dawn-dewed grass, chants the hymn
of interconnected
existence, a symphony
  played on the strings of the
universal web.

Each thought, like a star,
   burns in the solitude of
its own sky, crafting
light from the fuel of past
   knowledge, histories burned
    in the glow of now.

The hill-line catches,
    breaks the brittle morning light
   into beams that pierce
    my contemplative shade,
  illuminating doubts,
    sketching hope on stones.

This inner cosmos,
mapped yet mysterious,
defined yet so vast,
  where sacred dances with
   the secular: scenes meld,
meanings mix and merge.

  The fabric frays not
into disarray but forms
  new patterns, insights
      gleaned from the fray, the tear,
the break in monotony
that reshapes belief.

Threads, once orderly,
now entangle: complexity
is not disorder
but a higher form of
structure, demanding not
subjugation but respect.

  Each thread vibrates, a
string plucked in the spectrum of
    existence, echoing
across the valleys of
my mind, notes that combine
to form a melody.

In the threads: interwoven,
each whorl and twist,
  a narrative spun
in the dance of looms,
    where silence is
a partner to the thread.

Fractured light breaks
in shivers of dawn:
the hill-line shadows,
hunched and waiting,
    weave their own myth,
crisp in the brittle air.

Each leaf, a syllable,
  spoken in the gusts,
and winds, devout scribes,
  archive each twist
in the annals of the earth,
scriptures writ in soil.

Beneath the surface,
  roots gossip in the dark:
their murmured tales
spread like tendrils,
crossing boundaries,
in a whispering network.

Above: the sky arches,
  vast, an endless dome,
painting its azure thoughts
with clouds that drift -
freethinkers on the breeze,
  plotting their pathless maps.

Atoms, those tiny nomads,
migrate through forms,
  from stone to bloom to beast,
in endless transmutations,
each existence merely
a hostel in their journey.

The sun, a diligent alchemist,
transforms dew to vapor,
in a clear act of magic,
where science shakes hands
with the mystic, and both
acknowledge the wonder.

In this perpetual flux,
a leaf detaches, aloft,
whirling in its fall,
a ballet in descent,
and lands, a quiet echo
of the tree's release.

Rivers, those ancient travelers,
carry tales from the hills
down to the sea,
each drop a courier
of whispers, rumors,
and the deep's secrets.

Stones bear the weight
of history, uncomplaining:
their craggy faces,
etched by time's slow hand,
speak in the language
of permanence and change.

This fabric of existence,
tangled, yet precise,
demands no simplification,
resists easy patterns,
for its beauty lies
in intricate defiance.

Each breath, an exchange
between my inner wilds
and the world's vast lungs,
binds me to the tree,
the river, the stone,
in a silent pact of being.

So I traverse this landscape,
a map without boundaries,
where every marked line
is an invitation
to wander deeper
into the uncharted.

The wind whispers,
a confidant divulging
secrets in rustling tones,
and I lean in to listen,
a disciple of the moment,
hungry for its truths.

Here, where the mind
meets the matter,
reveries meld with mud,
and dreams sweep
across the terrain of the real,
blurring edges, erasing lines.

Each step a stitch
in the tapestry of days,
connecting color to color,
life to life,
in a network so vast,
it mirrors the cosmos.

In the weave, complexity:
a challenge to the eye
that seeks only simplicity,
and finds instead
a kaleidoscope
of interdependent tales.

Thus the journey winds,
    a path defined by its walking,
each footprint a statement,
a declaration of presence,
in this landscape where
every step alters the map.

Continuing, I find
that each decision branches,
  like the nerve-endings of thought,
or the veinings on a leaf,
    each choice a delta,
spreading into consequences.

And in this intricate maze,
where decisions weigh like stones,
and thoughts fly like leaves,
I find the threads of my being,
woven into the vastness,
part of the endless fabric.

Life spins on, a wheel,
and I, caught in its turning,
find solace in the spin,
joy in the whirl,
as every moment unfurls,
    each second a new thread.

The fabric sings,
  a chorale of fibers,
each note struck by the weft,
   the warp a melody playing
  across the loom of days,
music in the material.

As night draws its curtain,
the stars stitch silver
into the quilt of dusk,
  each point a puncture
where the dark is sewn
with the light of ancient fires.

Here, in the gathered gloom,
thoughts taper and twist,
finding paths through shadow,
each one a filament
  glowing briefly in the dark,
a fleeting firefly trail.

And so, through cycles
of light and absence,
the fabric persists,
worn but never weakened,
a testament to the resilience
    of woven destinies.

In this perpetual interplay,
the sacred and the mundane
merge, a dance of elements,
where the common dust
and the cosmos share
the same spiraling floor.

Thus, amid myriad threads,
my heart, a loom,
weaves the raw strands
of experience, fear,
hope, into a garment
fit to cloak my spirit.

In each thread, a pulse,
a beat of the universal heart,
resounding in the echo
of my own rhythms,
where the personal meets
the eternal, thread by thread.

As dawn returns,
shedding clarity in light,
I see the pattern anew,
each connection a bright line,
and all my fears,
mere shadows cast by truth.

The fabric, ever evolving,
asks not for completion,
but for participation
in its endless crafting,
a call to weave and be woven
into the vast tapestry of being.

Morning breaks: light spills,
its golden thread weaving,
across the russet earth,
each blade of grass bearing
the weight of dew: tiny
prisms fracturing light.

The hill-line, a rough sketch,
holds the horizon in check,
a boundary yet a beckoning:
each contour a narrative,
spoken in the tongue of
silences and spaces.

Trees stand in their quiet vigil,
roots delving into the dark
of soil: their life unseen,
yet palpable as the air is
with the scent of growth:
subtle, yet insistent.

A leaf falls: a slow drift,
a spiral through air, settled
by gravity's unyielding call:
so everything returns,
to the ground: to begin
again in a new guise.

Birdsong pierces the calm,
high notes scattered like
stars in a clear night sky:
each trill a pinpoint,
of sound in the vastness,
a claim staked on the day.

Wind gathers, sweeps,
carries with it tales
of distant mountains,
of valleys deep in shadow:
all connected, this fabric,
woven from breaths.

Air, thick with the promise
of rain: molecules ready
to coalesce, to fall, to feed
the thirsty earth, cycles
locked in a dance of
give and take: endless.

Clouds, vast canvases,
drift lazily: hosts of
shapes morphing, telling
their stories in the shape of
a dragon, then a ship,
sailing the blue deep.

The sun climbs, arcs,
its trajectory a slow burn
across the canvas of day,
each degree a marker of
time, invisible yet
undeniably felt.

Shadows stretch, elongate,
creep across the landscape,
their dark forms a cool
respite in the noonday glare,
a subtle shift of the
light's embrace.

Insects, tiny aviators,
buzz and whirl, their wings
a blur of motion, lives
lived in the span of a
day, yet full of
fierce urgency.

Flowers tilt their faces,
sunward: heliotropic
movements guided by
light, their petals vibrant
testaments to the power
of simple acts.

Roots tangle beneath the
surface, a silent network
of exchange: nutrients for
support, a subterranean
web of life, unseen but
foundational.

Leaves breathe, exhale,
their green surfaces
a vast factory of air,
transforming sunlight into
breathable gold, a gift
freely given, taken.

The cycle spins, a wheel
of life, death, rebirth,
each turn a revolution,
a reimagining of what
was, what is, what
might yet be.

Amidst this, a thought:
a strand in the vast web,
complex, interwoven,
its simplicity a guise
for deeper truths,
hidden yet real.

www.ingramcontent.com/pod-product-compliance
Lightning Source LLC
LaVergne TN
LVHW030636080426
835512LV00022B/3474